Looking Up, Looking Down

of related interest

Heavenly Stems and Earthly Branches – TianGan DiZhi
The Heart of Chinese Wisdom Traditions
Master Zhongxian Wu and Dr Karin Taylor Wu
Foreword by Fei BingXun
ISBN 978 1 84819 151 8 (HARDBACK)
ISBN 978 1 84819 208 9 (PAPERBACK)
eISBN 978 0 85701 158 9

Practical Zen for Health, Wealth and Mindfulness
Julian Daizan Skinner with Sarah Bladen
Foreword by Shinzan Miyamae
ISBN 978 1 84819 390 1
eISBN 978 0 85701 347 7

Calculating the BaZi
The GanZhi/Chinese Astrology Workbook
Karin Taylor Wu
Foreword by Master Zhongxian Wu
ISBN 978 1 84819 312 3
eISBN 978 0 85701 265 4

Seeking the Spirit of The Book of Change
8 Days to Mastering a Shamanic Yijing (I Ching) Prediction System
Master Zhongxian Wu
ISBN 978 1 84819 362 8
eISBN 978 0 85701 007 0

LOOKING UP, LOOKING DOWN

Guide to Classical Feng Shui

Reni Aleksandra Hagen
Translated from Norwegian by Peter Graves

SINGING DRAGON

LONDON AND PHILADELPHIA

First published in Norwegian by EUFEMIA, Oslo 2015
This edition first published in 2018
by Singing Dragon
73 Collier Street
London N1 9BE, UK
and
400 Market Street, Suite 400
Philadelphia, PA 19106, USA

www.jkp.com

Library of Congress Cataloging in Publication Data
A CIP catalog record for this book is available from the Library of Congress

British Library Cataloguing in Publication Data
A CIP catalogue record for this book is available from the British Library

ISBN 978 1 84819 398 7
eISBN 978 0 85701 359 0

Printed and bound in Great Britain

THANK YOU!

*A very special thank you to Grand Master Chan Kun Wah
for sharing the unique and precious knowledge of which
he is such an outstanding exponent!*

*Thank you, too, to all the clients who have invited me into their
houses and their lives. Without you I would never have gained
the rich experience necessary to write a book about feng shui.*

*And sincere thanks to all you students and course participants
– you have taught me more than you can know.*

CONTENTS

INTRODUCTION

Since you've found your way to this book, you must already have some kind of view of feng shui and be sufficiently curious to want to look into it further. More than likely, irrespective of how many books on feng shui you have read or browsed, you are both confused and baffled. That is not unusual. The fact of the matter is that there are few people who have any real idea of what feng shui actually is. The subject is multi-faceted and complex and most of the books on the market are full of misunderstood 'truths', as tends to happen when complex knowledge becomes common property.

You may, perhaps, have already flicked through the following pages and be wondering where all the gorgeous pictures have gone: this is a book about feng shui, after all, and books of this kind usually treat us to illustrations of everything from mystical dragons and gleaming amulets to colourful domestic interiors. The answer is that I want this book to be read, not just browsed.

I want the contents to give you – the reader – something more to think about, just as knowledge of this subject has given me so much to think about. It's not difficult to get hold of the pretty picture books. It is, however, more difficult to access their content, which is why I am offering text and almost nothing but text. I believe it is important to describe the wisdom of feng shui thoroughly and properly in words, and I believe it is possible to do so.

Feng shui is an ancient discipline that originated in the East and has been refined and developed over many thousands of years. Its roots lie in the observations of the earth and the heavens made by shamans and primitive peoples and in their shrewd and profound contemplation of processes to which people today pay scant attention. Feng shui is the oldest of all energy teachings and if one had to choose just one word to describe feng shui that word would be change. We know that we as human beings undergo physical and mental changes in the course of our lives; we remain the same, but we are also different. A garden changes character from season to season while remaining the same garden, but there is a huge difference between the lush flowering of summer and the wilted, frosted nature of the same place in late autumn. The globe as a whole undergoes changes, cyclical seasonal changes, but also big and small enduring changes, often in the wake of enormous natural catastrophes. And our globe is just a tiny speck among many other specks in the great universe, all of them also undergoing changes.

The foundation of the world's first natural science was a result of careful research into nature, natural phenomena and heavenly activity, combined with profound spiritual reflection and insight. Historical research shows that feng shui was practised as long as six thousand years ago. But feng shui is not only about understanding and creating change; it is itself a discipline in a continuous state of change. Hand in hand with the development of society, the discipline of feng shui has been subject to renewal and change. That is the nature of the discipline and that is why it can be practised as effectively in the modern cities of the West as in the Chinese countryside, and that is why it remains as effective today as in the distant past.

This ancient cultural heritage, however, just like many other things in many other parts of the world, has also been the victim of book-burning and persecution. The original discipline of feng shui was never common property. Rather the opposite: the complex nature of the subject was such that only a few became masters of it. The shaman or medicine man or medicine woman passed the baton on to the practitioner of feng shui, who was then able to provide information vital to a population that needed to be prepared for all kinds of wind and weather in order to avoid famine and disaster. Consequently, prediction was an important part of feng shui and, moreover, because of the discipline's superior accuracy and power, it was kept secret throughout much of history. Feng shui was a tool that gave the powerful even greater power, which to a considerable extent meant that the discipline and its practitioners in China belonged to the reigning emperor and the imperial court. This is the reason why some of the forms of feng shui – the authentic classical branches – are still called 'imperial feng shui'.

Imagine for a moment that you were the high king with the cleverest counsellor in the world at your side, and that this counsellor was the master of methods that guaranteed you and yours good health and longevity, prosperity, a prolific and good marriage, wealth and riches, honour, fame and success in statesmanship and war. Since you are a supreme ruler with a voracious appetite for more land, more power, more influence, more of everything, you will make very sure that the secret of your success will never reach the ears of unauthorised interlopers under any circumstances. You will see to it that these powerful and successful techniques are suitably guarded, concealed from outsiders and, just to be on the safe side, encoded to the point of incomprehensibility.

Feng shui records were paraphrased and encrypted in order to confuse outsiders – as were all important documents in those days. As the ancient papyrus scrolls were brought out, unrolled and studied in the modern age, many strange 'truths' about feng shui, which is a truly complex and wide-ranging teaching, began to be spread. Grand Master Chan Kun Wah, my teacher, has described the situation as follows: 'The texts were written down upside down and backwards and now there are so-called "masters" practising the discipline upside down and backwards.'

This is why so much peculiar feng shui is practised and why so much strange material is marketed as feng shui. Part of the purpose of this book is to bring some order to this chaos and to provide explanations. The original and serious discipline of feng shui deserves proper explication. And, I hope, clarification will help more people to enjoy the help that competent, serious practitioners of feng shui can give them.

Acupuncture and qi gong are therapeutic systems closely related to feng shui. Acupuncture is used to treat blockages in the body and, with the help of qi gong exercises, similar profoundly liberating results are achieved. Tai chi, acupressure, zone therapy and so on belong to the same rich tradition of holistic knowledge of health and wholeness. The systems are based on the idea that it is possible, when stagnation and imbalance are present in the physical functions, to open the way to a better flow of energy. The acupuncturist knows the points in the body's energy system that can be affected by extremely thin acupuncture needles. In a similar way, the movements, breathing and concentration exercises of qi gong have a profound effect on physical and psychic health. All the oriental holistic systems also have spiritual aspects – understandably, given that they are promoting wholeness.

We cannot see the body's meridians (energy pathways) and consequently when we first encountered Chinese medical systems and preventative health programmes such as qi gong and acupuncture we Westerners did not believe in any of this amazing knowledge. Acupuncture in particular, however, achieved recognition and popularity in the West relatively quickly, the reason being that sickness and health have become major issues for modern people with their misguided lifestyles. We want to be cured, but we have begun to question the culture of pill-popping: more and more of us are recognising that advanced Western medicine does not have all the answers and consequently we are looking elsewhere. Modern medicine is still very young indeed, whereas people have existed on this earth for many thousands of years. How did people manage earlier? For many people nowadays the pharmacy of nature and the self-healing capabilities inherent in our bodies have become an interesting and rewarding study.

So where does feng shui fit in? And why hasn't it found the same level of acceptance? Feng shui treats a house using the same principles that an acupuncturist applies to the human body. Without needles, of course. To someone who has never heard of feng shui or never bothered to consider the idea that everything is connected to everything else, this sounds like utter nonsense. In addition to which, since the sort of feng shui that has come to the West has a good deal of nonsense in its baggage, the situation is not an easy one for anyone who wants to explore the subject or who wants to pass on the knowledge.

I belong to both those categories. After a journey that has included a wide variety of feng shui courses, feng shui methods and feng shui books, I am now firmly convinced that I have found a unique and authentic source of wisdom. Classical feng shui itself, of course, contains different pathways, but after intense study and much practical feng shui work over the last ten years my experience tells me that I have come as close as it is possible to come to the source of authentic feng shui.

The fountain of knowledge I eventually discovered was the enthusiastic and profound teacher Chan Kun Wah and his classical form of feng shui known as 'Chue Style feng shui'. For me, this encounter has been of such great significance that even the top prizes in the lottery pale by comparison.

So stay with me – this handbook could be your key to a similar treasure chest.

1 WHAT IS FENG SHUI?

A direct translation of feng shui means 'wind water' – the alpha and omega of life, fertility and prosperity. According to an old text about feng shui, 'the energy of life – chi – is carried and spread by the wind and it is caught and held by water'. These words offer a good picture of the profundity of this fascinating subject.

FURNITURE WISDOM FROM CHINA?

There is wheat and there is chaff, and there is feng shui and there is feng shui. How can we separate the wheat from the chaff? What is the difference between feng shui and feng shui? Human beings are weak: we seek quick solutions which cost us as little as possible. Even though we know there is no such thing as a slimming pill that does what it promises, we still swallow it. All human beings desire security and well-being in their everyday lives, but for many people life is an arduous challenge. We seek meaning, happiness and, if possible, riches too. The lottery is a quick fix for the few – the very few – who have luck on their side. The rest of us carry on looking and possibly even stumble across magic formulae that promise gold and a Garden of Eden. We know that clever salesmen are cheating us time and again, but we nevertheless choose to believe their miracle cures.

When feng shui was launched in the West, its audience was one seeking quick fixes in pretty well all aspects of life. It is possible, as we know, to make money on anything and everything. The cost in this case has been the misuse, misunderstanding and ridicule of a great and serious discipline. Feng shui has become associated with wind chimes, money frogs and crystals; and, perhaps more than anything else, there are many people who believe it to be a kind of magical, zen-like approach to interior design. People are promised riches and happiness through the agency of mystical expedients and exotic figures. All you need to do is to sleep with your head to the north – or was it east? – and remove all pointed objects from the house. Not only are people being led astray, but they are paying good money to be led astray. It is impossible to exaggerate the disrespect being shown to the profound wisdom of Chinese philosophy and thought.

It is obviously difficult to see the point and seriousness of feng shui if you believe it to be a combination of exotic superstition and mystical interior design. I have heard the discipline described as 'furniture wisdom from China'. Feng shui has become modern and there is an ever-increasing number of people who call themselves feng shui experts on colour, shape and the positioning of tables and chairs. But feng shui is not about interior design; it is about energy. If you are an interior designer who chooses to study feng shui, you will be able to advise your clients both about the influences of energy and about nuances of colour – and there are many people who need help with both those things. But you do not need to know anything about colour codes or fashions in order to do a good feng shui job. You can be colour blind and still able to help your feng shui client to achieve a new and better life.

Three kinds of luck

The Chinese have always believed firmly that there is something we can call heaven luck: this is best described as 'fate' – the country and the family you are born into, as well as the gifts you are endowed with at birth, which, amazingly enough, can be decoded and analysed on the basis of the exact time you came into the world. Then there is man luck: this is the contribution made by your own efforts, what you do with your talents and possibilities. In other words, you cannot just put your trust in prayers, desires and affirmations, because will and action are also required. The third kind of luck is earth luck, which has to do with the conditions and circumstances of your place of residence and its surroundings – in other words, feng shui!

Those who have studied feng shui as a discipline know that feng shui is not magic. The achievement of good feng shui – that is, having good possibilities in life rather than many major problems and challenges – demands alertness and effort. A skilled feng shui practitioner can provide the alertness; the effort comes from the client, who must take the time and make the effort to follow the advice given by the feng shui consultant.

And there are times when the results really can be magical, but that is a different matter.

A house is a house is a house...

To understand what feng shui is, we must first ask ourselves the question 'What is a house, a place of residence?' Even though our house/place of residence means a great deal to us, very few people actually ask that question. We think of buildings, whether they be castles, commercial buildings, houses or flats, garages or woodsheds, as places with walls, roofs, windows and doors. In our private lives our places of residence fulfil our need for somewhere to eat, sleep, enjoy ourselves and look after ourselves and each other: we need keys, safety and certainty. And the address is important to some people, as is the view, the size, the appearance and the status.

But what is a residence over and above all that, because it is undoubtedly something more? It takes more than just a house key for us to be in a position to unlock a greater understanding of what is meant by a residence. The home we grow up in, and later the home we ourselves create as adults and fill with a new family, is like a physical shell that protects our private sphere from the outside world. It is not just a physical shell, however; it is also a layer of energy surrounding all the other layers of energy of which we are made up. It is a body of energy we are one with and it is shaped and furnished and decorated by us. But not only do we shape it; it – in quite unique ways – also shapes us. People in every culture apart from our Western culture are familiar with the concept of life energy. It is the force that sustains us, that makes us able to move around on our two legs and smile, flirt, work, love and squabble. Every living thing on this planet is sustained by life energy. The alternative to a flourishing plant is a wilting plant, and a wilting plant is either dead or close to death. If you have ever seen someone who is dead, you will have seen what happens when life energy has departed.

Chi – the breath of life

The Chinese call this energy chi or qi, as in qi gong. In India the term for the same thing is prana, the Japanese say ki, and in Indian culture and language it is called nipi, just to give a few examples. The breath of life, or life energy, is the closest we can come in translation in our part of the world. But the important thing to recognise is that a house also needs good life energy. Whether it stands on blocks of stone, on piles, on solid foundations or straight on the ground, it is there to serve us day and night. Our place of shelter provides us with whatever it has by way of good or bad protection from wind and weather, a greater or lesser degree of security, and the chance to draw breath and recharge before returning to the struggle.

We all know that the quality of our lives depends on the level of energy and beneficial flow in our bodies, but it is also linked to the level of energy and flow in the important layer with which we surround ourselves – in other words, our home. It is this that is the starting point for all classical feng shui.

So a house is only apparently a shell. Before we move in, it is empty of furniture and other objects, but it is already full of air and has already drawn in life energy from its surroundings. It absorbs and then offers us a blend of everything going on around it, whether that is good fresh air, pollution, disruptive noise, pleasing calm, forest scents, exhaust fumes or general hustle and bustle. In order to understand what feng shui is really about, we need to spend some time on both the idea and the experience of a house being a living organism with a unique character. Those who have studied and practised feng shui know this from experience. A place of residence offers both challenges and opportunities, and the factors that decide how fortunate our choice of home is are associated with the energy influences of the architecture of the house and its location. Does the house have access to good chi? Does it have good support? Is the life energy properly taken care of? Is fresh chi allowed into the whole house, into all the rooms and every corner?

Sang chi, sit chi, sat chi

There are different kinds of chi. There is life-giving energy (sang chi), draining energy (sit chi) and energy that is directly negative (sat chi). Being in the right place at the right time involves knowing how to capture the good, life-giving energy and to avoid and protect yourself against draining, unfavourable and negative energies and influences. This is what feng shui is about: the art of producing the best surroundings that will work to our advantage while avoiding the influences of the worst.

What this means in real life is that you must make very conscious use of all your senses when choosing a place of residence. Avoid the sat chi that comes from rubbish dumps, vehicle scrapyards, traffic noise, foul-smelling industries with their filth and noise, airfields, jagged and threatening mountains, run-down neighbouring buildings, transformers, ugly lamp-posts and the sharp corners of other buildings. Also be careful about sit chi, that is to say the kind of conditions around your house that means that energy runs away from it. Another situation that can cause energy to drain away is when it has not been channelled accurately to your house and finds its way to a neighbour's place instead. A further circumstance that can lead to energy draining away is when the house does not have good enough support from its surroundings.

Sang chi: nourishing; good and supportive
influence. 'Sang' means life-giving.

Sat chi: negative, unfavourable, ugly
influence. 'Sat' means poisonous.

Sit chi: draining elements; the energy is
led away. 'Sit' means draining.

The best precondition for good feng shui is good support on all sides, views out onto beautiful and fertile surroundings along with an absence of negative sat chi, also known as 'poison arrows', especially any arrows that point directly at the mouth of the house (the entrance door) and the spine (the middle of the back of the house).

The best feng shui is achieved when life energy reaches the house in a naturally curving and balanced way, by which is meant that the chi should not travel towards the entrance in a straight line (more about this in Chapter 4).

All of these things are visual influences and consequently easy to take into account when choosing a house – in so far as choice is an option, of course. It is usually possible to do something about visual influences of this kind: remove or cover sat chi; strengthen and improve the support around and in the house in order to counteract sit chi; and, for example, where a line is too straight and abrupt, construct curves in order to achieve sang chi.

But there are also invisible influences on energy. There is slow-working earth energy and there is rapid and unrelenting heaven energy. Human beings and all living things are caught between and subject to these powerful forces. Some people are lucky and end up in good houses with good energy around them. In reality, given where and how we live crowded together in towns, few people enjoy the best feng shui and there will always be challenging aspects. The question then becomes what are the challenges the building is creating in a permanent sense and what does this imply for the specific individual who lives there or is about to move in. Your earth luck is connected with heaven luck, so don't believe that it was you and you alone (man luck) who chose the residence for yourself. It is equally a case of the residence choosing you.

We inhale air, but we don't see it. Life energy supports us even though it is invisible to us. It is a reality in everything around us even though we don't see it. It is enormous and fills the whole universe. Life energy is behind the cycles and movements in the vastness of the heavens above us – in the movements and life of the sun, the moon and the planets and their influence on earthly cycles: flood tides and ebb tides, the seasons of the year, human life. The influences of heaven energy are also associated with the passage of time, with changes in time, with the characteristics of time, and they in turn have an effect on spatial issues: the characteristics of a given area and a given residence, for instance, are not the same today as they were a hundred years ago. And in a hundred years' time they will again be new and different. Change is life energy in motion and this motion, in its turn, creates new changes. We can see this in the human body: its form changes throughout life and there can be no doubt that there is a mutual dynamic at work in the interplay between energy and form, from youth with growth and activity, to middle and old age with decline and a diminished level of mobility.

Earthly life energy has to do with the environment around us, and it is also about the soil itself. A true master of feng shui smells and tastes the soil where a client is considering setting up a home. Earth chi deals with the quality of the landscape around us, the influence of mountains, rivers, sea, forests and other vegetation. It also takes account of subterranean influences, such as water courses or radiation. Earth energy is usually slow and sluggish, but because it is invisible we tend not to notice it so much.

Ecology

The foundation of authentic classical feng shui is based on a holistic understanding of nature. It has been called the oldest ecological teaching in the world. On this remarkable but tiny little earth of ours we are subject to the influence of cosmic forces in the vastness of space around us. The study of heaven and earth is ancient and the knowledge that was collected and processed is still alive in Chinese medicine, culture, philosophy and the art of living. The wisdom of Taoism, the effectiveness of acupuncture, the practice of herbal medicine by barefoot doctors, the holistic understanding of man as part of something bigger – all this is based on shamanistic observations of nature and the cosmos, of physics and biology, meteorology and geography, of the behaviour and well-being of animals and humankind. The knowledge in Taoism and feng shui about everything that goes on around us is enormous and rests on thousands of years of profound examination of the great existential questions.

In China this has led to a firmly held world view that everything is connected. Respect and reverence for nature and its energy laws are embedded in the culture and still in the best of health.

I Ching, which is the oldest collection of wisdom texts in the world as well as being the oldest and most used oracle, is a good example of the kind of time span and historical perspective we are dealing with. (It is still in use today.) The earliest known historical traces of this collection of profound and advanced knowledge may be dated back to 4000 to 6000 BC, and in our own day modern researchers are discovering striking connections between the natural sciences and the mystical patterns of I Ching.

Both in China and in the West feng shui is the least widespread and least known branch of this rich tradition of knowledge. A literal translation of feng shui is 'wind water'. As the name suggests, it is a discipline that is concerned with the powerful forces of nature that surround us. Both wind and water form landscape. Human beings have always sought shelter from the wind and been completely dependent on water. In earlier times, finding places to live that could offer protection against powerful natural forces at the same time as providing fertile soil and guaranteed crops was utterly decisive for human life and survival. Feng shui gives us access to a language which enables us to understand and communicate better with nature.

There are, for instance, only a few people who have any idea of the deep connection between the season and the heaven direction and why this is important knowledge. Or that the season and heaven direction have a connection in terms of energy with the cycles in human life and the rhythm of the day. In feng shui these connections and values are decoded and expressed in the vast body of knowledge contained in I Ching. All the information about all the directions, all the shifts in cycles great and small, are gathered in 64 hexagrams, each consisting of six lines. A hexagram consists of two trigrams (three lines). There are eight trigrams, each made up of unbroken and broken lines, and each trigram is said to contain all the essential information about existence.

The eight *trigrams* that tell about nature, heaven directions, the cycles of the year and of the day and about all aspects of human life.

Three lines – trigrams full of life

In Chinese energy teaching, all parts of the body, all organs, human functions and characteristics, as well as important areas of life, are linked with a trigram. Feng shui experts and practitioners of Chinese medicine, acupuncturists, chi gong masters and others all share this knowledge. A trigram is made up of three lines which can either be broken or unbroken: the unbroken lines are yang (active, agent), the broken are yin (passive, accepting). By combining yin and yang lines it is possible to produce eight different trigrams. Each of them represents a phenomenon in nature, various aspects of existence, what it means to be human, and also various parts of the body – physical organs and so on.

Each of the eight trigrams also represents a member of the family and, importantly, each is connected to one of the five elements – wood, fire, earth, metal and water. All of these are of great significance and are used and understood widely in feng shui and Chinese medicine.

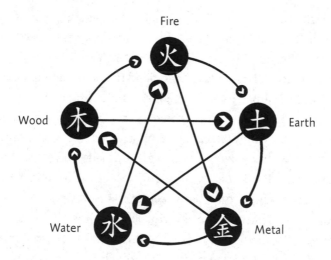

Copyright © Thomas Hagen Kaldhol

Knowledge of the trigrams and elements are powerful tools in the hands of the feng shui expert, as is an understanding that every place of residence is like a living organism, a body that needs nourishment. The supply of nourishment affects the way the inhabitants of a house will perform in life and what their lives will be like. Since the trigrams and elements in the house are associated with particular directions, and houses are positioned and shaped in all kinds of ways, each particular house will affect the lives of its occupants in a unique manner. The form of the house (layout, positioning of doors, etc.) and the direction in which it is placed will tell us which members of the family are nourished or not nourished and how well or badly all aspects of life are nurtured by the actual structure of the house. There will be more about the trigrams and the five elements in Chapter 4.

FENG SHUI IN ACTION

I'm on my way to a feng shui consultation. It's for a woman who has recently been given a diagnosis so serious that she needs to consider whether to adapt her house to make it accessible for someone who is disabled or to sell it and find somewhere new and more suitable. I'm excited at the idea of meeting someone who, despite gloomy prospects, is taking control of their life situation in such a creative and active way. She has read the same feng shui books as I have and, like me, has put them aside in frustration but without discarding the idea that feng shui must have something to offer. That is how some of us react, as a result perhaps of some sort of recognition: it may be that every time we read about three-legged money frogs, lucky coins, crystal prisms, dragon dogs and wind chimes we hear a distant echo of something quite different.

My client has decided to call in feng shui expertise in order to ensure she has the best quality of life possible. She has already been in contact with an architect and been given various suggestions regarding special solutions in any new house.

She lives in a large house, but it's old and she may find it imposes serious limitations on her life if or when she becomes very dependent on care.

I sit in the car reflecting on the seriousness of the situation into which I am being invited and the responsibility being placed on me. Fortunately, the woman in question is not someone who subscribes to the delusion that feng shui is a branch of sorcery and that I will turn up with a bag full of magic bits and pieces and hocus-pocus solutions to all her pains and problems.

When I was new to the business, I would go to a new client feeling more than a little nervous; the feng shui compass felt so powerful and the subject itself was so vast and there were so many things to think about. I took my commissions just as seriously then as now, but I have noticed that the deeper I go into the discipline, the greater the challenges and seriousness of the commissions become. At the same time I am amazed by my own sense of becoming more and more confident. I am confident that I am getting exactly the challenges I should be getting and that my client is receiving precisely the feng shui help he or she needs or is ready for. And after almost ten years as an active practitioner of the discipline I am utterly convinced that this unique body of knowledge can change people's lives in important ways.

'Is there something the matter with the house?'

Most of the people who consult me are people wanting help to achieve clarity at some kind of impasse in their lives. They have tried many things and have ended up wondering, 'Is there something the matter with the house?' It's become quite popular these days to have someone come to the house to purify things in a spiritual sense. In many cases one can imagine that elementary feng shui would have been just as much help.

Feng shui includes an understanding of both visible and invisible influences. In the everyday practice of the discipline the invisible influences do not involve unquiet souls; on the other hand, the unfavourable effects of elements, perhaps magnified by the architecture of the house or quite simply by a mirror, can have a powerful impact on the lives of the occupants and be experienced as unpleasant and threatening. (A mirror, of course, hangs there all day and all night and it both reflects and multiplies!) There are also occasions when no one notices anything, but the unfavourable effect or influence is present all the same and will in time become manifest in the form of conflicts, financial problems, health issues and many other things.

On the basis of a description provided by my new client, I know in advance where I should focus my attention when I start work. First of all I try to find out whether there is 'something the matter with the house' and afterwards to work out whether the house will be suitable for her in the future. In all probability she will need adapted housing, which makes it all the more important that the house gives her as much support as possible. When designing a new house, it is perfectly possible to use feng shui to supply supportive energy and thus effectively tailor the residence to its occupants. Since this means taking energy flows into consideration, such adaptations would actually be invisible.

The basic energies
Every house needs a supply of fresh life energy in the same way as we need to fill our lungs with fresh air. We don't think about it every time we draw breath because breathing is such an everyday matter, but we are well aware that if the supply of air runs out and we cannot breathe we will be asphyxiated. We also know that unclean air is not good for us.

The same thing holds true for the house in which we live and work: it has to be allowed to breathe. What this means in practice is that it must have a supply of fresh life energy. In addition to the house itself, this also applies to the plot on which it stands – that too needs a life-giving supply of fresh energy. The gateway to the house and the entrance door are of great importance: there should be a good flow of energy to the property; the gateway should not be open to or surrounded by negative influences from the surroundings; the entrance door must get a good supply of energy and open in a direction which enables the supply of 'nourishment' to be appropriate to the needs of the particular house. It is possible to reveal all this by using relatively simple methods to discover what kind of basic energy the house has.

The basic energy in a house can be one of 64 types depending on the direction in which the house is sited and where the entrance door is. We have four cardinal directions – main directions – and four sub-cardinal directions. North, south, east and west are cardinal directions whereas north-east, south-east, south-west and north-west are sub-cardinals. Just as each season of the year has its unique quality, the different directions also have their own characteristics. We all know what spring does for us: we see growth and new life around us as the green leaves burst forth and we feel how spring energy gives us the courage, desire and will to press forward with new efforts. We find the same energy in the east and it is from there that we receive new and fresh replenishment every single morning when the sun rises – as long as the direction is not blocked by dense woods or building. Ideally, the house should also be able to let this fresh energy in through the windows and doors. A house that bathes in energy from the east, particularly if it can open up to this fresh energy, is a house that will inspire creativity and new ideas.

Cardinal directions: the four main directions that most of us are familiar with. The sun rises in the **east**, is at its highest point in the **south**, goes down in the **west** and is invisible to us in the **north**. They also correspond to the seasons of the year and are logically connected with the five elements and with the main phases of human life.

Sub-cardinal directions are connected with the transitional phases between the seasons. In terms of elements, they are a mixture of the before- and after-direction. The strong earth characteristics in the **north-east** and **south-west** make these two sub-cardinal directions 'earth directions'. In human life they correspond to the transition between phases of life.

Direction	Season	Element	Character	Life phase
north-east	late winter	earth	spirituality	life in womb
east	spring	wood	growth	childhood
south-east	early summer	wood	exploration	puberty
south	summer	fire	maturation	youth
south-west	late summer	earth	care	young adult
west	autumn	metal	responsibility	adult
north-west	late autumn	metal	authority	middle age
north	winter	water	reflection	old age/ new life

As in heaven, so on earth... Thus the 64 different forms of basic energy on the plot on which the house stands are associated with directions, and the direction in which the house faces, together with the positioning of the entrance door, determines what kind of energy enters the house. And it is this that determines which bigger and more powerful – cosmic – influences the house will attract to itself. The stars in the constellation of the Plough constitute the starting point for calculating the basic energies of a residence. Each of them represents a specific shape that is in harmony with a similar (mountain) shape on our Earth. Each individual shape is connected with something either positive or negative: a long and good life, prosperity, good health, bad luck and misfortune, conflicts and disagreements, dissipation and addiction, unpredictable or haunting energy and so on. To a greater or lesser extent our lives are influenced by one or more of these phenomena, and the house we inhabit is a contributory factor. The kitchen, the bedrooms and the study should preferably be filled with good basic energies. Bad energies can be left where they do least damage – for instance, in the laundry room, closet and rooms that are rarely used.

In feng shui these phenomena are associated with nine different forms of energy, both visible and invisible. Each form is linked in turn with one of the stars in the Plough, which has only seven visible stars, but there are also two which are not visible to the naked eye. At some point in the past they must have been visible in the sky because the wise shamans of old in the East recorded their observations of them.

If, for instance, you are unfortunate and fate causes addictive energies to be directed at a part of the house where excellent food and drink are served, things can easily degenerate into wild parties. Or there may be unfavourable energy in an area where there is also a steep staircase. You are fortunate if you have romantic energies in the bedroom or career and money energy in your home office. Everyday life teaches us, however, that no one has everything and most of us need something to sharpen up our act. Adversity is not necessarily damaging; indeed, we can learn from it. If, however, the basic energies are too challenging, life will be strenuous and tiring, and that is when professional feng shui analysis will be useful.

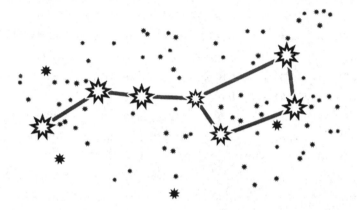

Copyright © Nevada31/Depositphotos.com

Throughout the ages the Plough has been an important constellation for seafarers and others who have needed a safe method of finding their position and navigating. The handle of the Plough always points in the direction that corresponds to the current season.

Good basic energies can be reinforced and bad ones weakened, though they will still be present. The basic energies of a house are fixed and permanent and can only be altered if the entrance door is complete repositioned. If the situation is really bad and the usage of the rooms in the house cannot be changed, there are good reasons to consider moving the entrance door. This is obviously impossible in the case of flats and seldom possible in the case of terraced housing.

Heaven energies

Feng shui is not only a matter of direction and space; it also involves time, which means that in addition to the basic energy of the house, there will also be a specific temporal energy, which is composed of the five elements. These are heaven influences of a different character to the basic energies referred to above. According to Chinese metaphysical thinking, the five elements govern and set their stamp on all life and all the processes on earth, and feng shui utilises knowledge of them in order to create a good and effective balance. There are 16 different ways the five elements work on a house. These can sometimes be propitious, in which case it is good for us to be aware of them and thus able to take advantage. Sometimes, however, they are unfavourable, in which case they should and can be counteracted. If we are able to assess the feng shui in a temporal sense, it means we are in a position to ascertain when a house is subject to good or less good influences. A house may have the potential for prosperity, for careers, for ill health and so on, and in particular years and months this influence will be more marked. When we know this, we can take appropriate measures.

Heaven energies are fast energies. Their effects can be hard and brutal, but they can also be exploited or countered equally quickly by using remedies offered by the five elements. Constellations of the five elements are positioned differently in different houses and the effect they have depends on how a house is laid out (the use of the rooms) and furnished in terms of shapes and colours. But heaven energies are not only inherently fast; they also change at relatively short intervals – seen in the perspective of the long time span of humanity, the Earth and the Milky Way. The big feng shui cycle is a cycle of 180 years, which is divided into an 'upper' and a 'lower' period, each of 90 years. These are then further divided into shorter periods of varying lengths.

In popular feng shui literature you will read that all of these periods are of 20 years – that is quite simply a result of defective knowledge of yin and yang.

If you remain in the same house from birth to death, you will have experienced three or four distinct 'energy periods' during which the five elements will have affected your house and your life in very different ways. More information about the five elements will be found in Chapter 4.

In front and behind

On arriving at the house in which my client lives, I slow down in good time in order to orient myself with regard to the directions and to 'tune in' to what is happening around the property.

Outside I note a couple of dominant and ugly lamp posts as well as the fact that the house has poor protection from the busy road behind it. The driveway continues past the house to a garage and a small annex for guests farther into the plot.

This property used to be a farm and the combination of additions and divisions to the original buildings has resulted in clumsy solutions. There is, for instance, no obvious path to the entrance door of the house I am visiting. As I mentioned earlier, houses must have a proper opportunity to breathe and on my way in I wonder how this house could possibly breathe life into someone who is ill. Fortunately, though, the main door is at the front of the house so at least the face of the building is obvious.

This is not always the case. For various reasons many houses have the main door at the back. This is a contradiction, for in feng shui terms the spine is at the back and we neither have eyes in the back of our necks and nor can we consume food and drink from that side. On the other hand, however, we do need to be able to lean back in the secure knowledge that there is good support behind us.

If the house does not supply that kind of support, its occupants will frequently experience an absence of support in their lives. The front represents the future and our possibilities in life, whereas the back represents the past, support and health. We receive and make use of new possibilities and dispose of what we no longer want. If what is in front of us is closed off, it's possible that few new possibilities will enter our lives. Think of the human body for a moment and imagine that the mouth was placed at the back where we dispose of what we no longer want – you can see at once what a problem that poses. Houses with their entrance doors at the back are challenging.

A closed-off future

Immediately in front of this house there is a great, impressive tree that has been there for ages. But it masks the magnificent view that can be enjoyed from anywhere else on the property but not from the house! In real life the future is in front of us, which is why feng shui states that a blockage in front of a house can affect our future prospects. The woman in this house is concerned about her future prospects now she has been diagnosed as having a serious health problem. I look at the house and realise that various extensions have created gaps and irregularities, which means that one or more of the eight trigrams is not in place. This in turn means that there are certain aspects that the house is not taking care of. Thus, even before going inside the house, I have registered and noted a whole list of things that will have to be dealt with.

With the help of measurements taken with my feng shui compass, I am able to find more pieces of the puzzle. Together with my client, I work my way systematically though the house and we find both visible and invisible explanations for things that have happened in the family. But the most important thing now is to discover what kind of effect the house will have on her in the particular life situation in which she now finds herself. There is much that can be done without incurring heavy costs, and since this house is resting on an energy that fits this individual like a glove, I recommend that she remains there and gets help to make the necessary adaptations in view of her future as a disabled person.

The alternative would be a new house, and since my client finds that idea attractive, we drive to a new housing development in the area. The building plot available to her there will create problems and limitations (the basic energies) with regard to the positioning of the house. After various measurements and calculations it becomes quite obvious that a house in this location will be very unlikely to achieve good feng shui and, given the situation she is in, good feng shui is the highest priority when it comes to determining the quality of her life in the coming years.

Earth luck and 'green fingers'

I return home after my visit with a full notebook of observations, measurements, discussion points and impressions. What I now have in front of me is another exciting phase of the feng shui commission – computations and calculations, the uncovering of further energy connections, and the writing of my report. The latter should preferably have an encouraging rather than a discouraging tone.

Unfortunately, the discoveries you make as a feng shui consultant are often not very optimistic. The connections between the place of residence and the challenges people face are striking and can be discouraging. But can we really expect anything other than problems, both small and large, when houses are planned, designed and built without any understanding of the way houses affect us?

Anyone who is successful at cultivating pot plants knows that having 'green fingers' is all about creating the proper growing conditions for the particular plant: right size pot, right soil, right amount of light, right temperature, right doses of feed, right amount of water and so on. Similarly, even quite elementary knowledge of the importance of our surroundings can create better conditions for each and every one of us – in other words, better earth luck: unbroken house surfaces, healthy house bodies, good support all round, a healthy supply of life energy, the absence of negative influences, particularly those that point towards the entrance door and the spine of the house. Very few of us are fortunate enough to enjoy immediate good feng shui from what the housing market offers us. But we can make the best of the circumstances in which we find ourselves – and that is where feng shui and feng shui expertise comes into the picture.

WIND AND WATER

The original name of the discipline was *ham jyy* (Cantonese pronunciation), which literally means 'looking up, looking down'. Once again, we have associations and connections with ancient shamanic wisdom. Above us is the sky and all its constellations, which can tell us about heaven luck; under us we have the earth where we walk, live and work, and this can offer good or bad earth luck. Between these two is everything that lives, where eco-communities have their own laws. And among the laws in nature are the fixed laws that life energy follows and that everything alive is part of. Among all living things, humankind is the species with a special ability to organise itself and use its will, talent and creativity to shape development. For good or for bad, as we know.

What is it about wind and water that make them such important phenomena for our man luck here on earth? After all, fire and heat are also necessary for life and growth. And we need soil in order to cultivate things, not to mention the importance of the plant and animal kingdoms, from which we get all the resources that provide us with food. So what's so important about wind and water?

Wind and water are the alpha and omega of life, fertility and welfare. Life energy – chi – is carried and spread by the wind, and it is caught and held by water. This sentence gives us a good image of the profundity of feng shui. Shelter from the wind provides a better basis for life and growth, and proximity to water means that the foundations for future generations can be laid down. A tiny seed that is swept away by the wind and lands among the scorching sands of the desert has very little hope of sprouting. But if the wind blows that seed in another direction and it lands beside a lake, there is a good chance that it will shoot, grow, take root and propagate. Spread by the wind and held by the water.

We can picture it all and see the seed, the desert, the water and small shoots. And we can transfer this image to other parts of existence: safe surroundings, fertility, crops, full bellies, happy children, well-being, development, growth and all the possibilities for many generations.

Life energy is subject to the same laws, but it is invisible to the naked eye, which is why we have major problems with genuinely accepting its existence. We only accept what we can see and understand – in spite of the fact that we live in an age in which we are constantly surrounded by mysteries: we can send text messages to the other side of the globe and they can be read by the recipient in Kuala Lumpur just a few seconds after we've sent them from our mobile while standing on a square in Edinburgh. We can be walking along Oxford Street in London and suddenly the screen on our mobile is filled with a photo taken just a minute before in Hawaii. Or while sitting in the corner of the sofa we send a document to the printer. Wirelessly! The pages of my manuscript fly invisibly through walls and rooms and end up as a pile of paper on the printer. How does it happen? What kind of seven-league boots are at work here? It's magic, quite simply magic. But when you use that kind of mysterious, incomprehensible, magic technology no one comes out with sarcastic comments such as 'You don't really believe in that, do you?' We don't understand what is happening, but we accept it. Not only do we accept it, but we take it as self-evident, to such an extent that we are frustrated and end up in a bad mood if we can't immediately and seamlessly get online with our children on their way up Kilimanjaro or contact our grandchildren who are enjoying their advanced studies in a hammock in deepest Amazonia. We take the advantages, forget the magic and only relate to the amazing usefulness.

The shamans and ancient sages had a more profound understanding than modern experts in mobile and wireless technology. They did not feel that there was something else between heaven and earth. They had no doubts about it. They knew from their observations, their calculations and their profound insights. The most ancient research project in the world penetrates deeply and extensively into the knowledge and significance of life energy. In our day this knowledge is restricted to just a few modern sages, a handful of surviving feng shui masters.

A universal treasure chest
The discipline of classical feng shui is not based on religious assumptions or superstition, nor is it based on magic spells or the use of special objects. After a feng shui consultation your house will not need to be filled up with even more things.

Rather the reverse: good feng shui is not necessarily visible. It is, perhaps, at its very best when it cannot be seen at all. Nor do you need to feel it. What is important is that you notice the difference in the life you are living. Classical feng shui is based completely on well-tried scientific observations and analyses. And the subject of all this research is primarily the decisive force around us – what we call chi or life energy. Feng shui is pure logic and reason and you don't need to hold a special belief or attitude for a feng shui approach or cure to work. When the discipline is practised seriously and according to classical principles, nothing is left to intuition, guesswork or conjecture.

The fact that feng shui originated in the East and developed within the context of Chinese culture and tradition does not mean that it is something distant and alien and of no use to us in the modern West. Life energy is universal and the roots of feng shui are so ancient that we can consider it a cultural inheritance relevant to all of us. Feng shui can be practised everywhere in the world, in houses, cabins, apartments, business premises, shopping centres, towns and villages, in the West as much as in the East. There is no need to learn Chinese and there is no need to know anything at all about Buddhism, Taoism or Confucianism in order to enjoy the usefulness and happiness that classical feng shui can bring to the quality of your life. The same is true should you want to study the discipline itself. The only thing you need to know is that it is an extensive and demanding discipline and you will be profoundly disappointed if you think that studying it merely consists of colour codes and magic formulae.

But if you are curious to learn what feng shui is and what lies at the root of the powerful methods the discipline involves, it is sensible to take a closer look at its background and at its main pillars. In other words, to examine the foundations of the discipline and to see what a practitioner has to offer.

The order of all things

Most people have heard of yin and yang and may even have the symbol as a brooch, a fridge magnet or a poster. Very few people, however, understand the real profundity of the symbol. The Western mind views yin and yang as black and white, as opposite poles, as contrasts. Yin and yang are opposites – two opposite forces in the universe – but the important point is that they are also mutually dependent on one another: one cannot exist without the other. Night would not exist without day, the sunny side would not exist if there wasn't also a shady side, depth would not exist unless there was height, and so on.

Yin stands for the feminine principle – mother earth, the moon, water, cold, darkness, passivity, receptivity, weight, peace, motionlessness, what is low, flat, soft. Yang stands for the masculine principle – the sky, sun, fire, heat, light, activity, giving and bestowing, lightness, movement, what is high, towering, hard.

Copyright © Janabehr, Dreamstime.com

Yin and yang in perfect balance.

In feng shui, knowledge of yin and yang plays an absolutely fundamental and decisive role. To the Chinese, who have been familiar with these insights for millennia, not only the symbol but also the content and meaning of the concept are self-evident in everyday life. To the people of China, and in every corner of everything that is Chinese, yin and yang stand for the order of all things. Everything in existence is supported by the relationship between yin and yang – everything and at all times. When you study Chinese history and philosophy, it becomes clear how holistic thinking and the aspiration for harmony and balance have been both the aim and the means in the great empire throughout the ages. Stability has been important at all costs.

When we look at bodies and lifestyle, we can clearly see that lack of harmony and balance has a cost. The Chinese have always known that an imbalance in the body's energy system leads to blockages which provide fertile soil for illness. Knowledge of yin and yang is utterly central to Chinese medicine, both for diagnosis and for treatment.

The organs in the body are either yin or yang. The organs that are characterised as yin are those that have the ability to accommodate and hold on to things, in contrast to those organs that produce and transport things. Just as in the environment all around us, what is at work is a clever system in which too much or too little in one place has consequences in another place. When cold refuses to release its grip and great masses of snow lie in the mountains far into spring, on the day that the heat of sun and summer suddenly takes over there are catastrophic consequences in the countryside below.

Life energy should, at best, be in balance, but it can sometimes be too yin and sometimes too yang. Someone who is depressed, for instance, is under the influence of yin energy, which grows stronger and drags the sufferer down even more. When a depressed individual receives acupuncture, the needles are placed at points which slowly but surely raise the sufferer up again.

In feng shui yin and yang are decisive for an understanding of time and space. Yin and yang describe directions and also tell us about the cycles of the seasons and the cycle of the day. Yin and yang explain the cycles of nature, the cycles in human life and everything else that is born, lives and dies. If we think of the symbol as an expression of the 24 hours of day and night, the point of intersection where yang (white) takes over from yin (black) at the bottom of the symbol would mark the very start of the dawning of the new day. Yang represents, as we've said, light, sun, day, warmth. The symbol illustrates quite clearly how it grows lighter through the morning and how the day reaches its zenith at noon. And at that point yin takes over and the day begins to wind down through afternoon until it once again reaches eventide and then the hours of night.

As we can see, day is lying in wait in the darkness of night, and the darkness of night is waiting its turn however bright and sunny the day may be. At the very moment yang is at its strongest, yin stands ready to take over the baton. And vice versa. Such is the course of nature and such, too, is human life, from foetus and new-born through childhood, youth, adulthood, middle age, old age and death. And it is the same with the seasons and with all natural phenomena. Even though modern people may have forgotten, they too are a part of nature and yin and yang is manifested very clearly in life and in the production of new life: yin and yang, woman and man, seek out and find one another and new life and new generations are created. That is what happens with all the vast and varied number of natural species on the Earth. Yin always seeks yang and yang always seeks yin, and the meeting between the two is the precondition for all fertility, all growth and all varieties of change. Yin and yang are the very heartbeat of everything that exists. Advanced methods of feng shui never lose sight of this and the aim of surveying and providing remedies for a house is to create or re-establish a balance between yin and yang to lead to a good and lasting change for the better.

What is it that leads to the universal dance of yin and yang? What are the forces that constantly attract and repel one another and create new life? Yin is not just yin and yang is not just yang – both forces accommodate many different processes. The Chinese have described this with the help of the theory of the five elements.

Five life processes

The ancient shamans explained yin and yang and the whole of existence with the help of the cycles of nature. The Chinese have preserved this knowledge, developed it further in Taoism and still live according to it. Yin and yang contain the opposing forces that contribute to the constant cyclical process of growth and change. These forces are primarily the two pairs – fire and water, wood and metal. Water extinguishes fire, metal cuts wood. These are the elements with which humankind has lived in a state of strong dependence throughout the whole of history. We need water in order to survive and to be able to cultivate things. All growth also presupposes the right temperature, so a balanced relationship between fire and water is of considerable significance. Growth, however, is also dependent on a contribution by metal, which trims and cuts. Metal tools are the result of a clever use of fire and water.

In other words, the four basic elements form the precondition for life and survival and are also the cornerstones of the development of civilisation. But there is also a fifth element – earth – which relates to all of these four and is essential for all life. Wood is planted in earth and earth has to be watered in order to be fruitful. The water element is yin, the fire is yang. Nothing can grow without the appropriate heat. Earth would be infertile without water and fire.

We reap a rich harvest of what grows immediately above and immediately below the surface of the earth. And there is more for us deeper down, where valuable metals and minerals are created. Wherever there are deposits of metal there is always water, and where there is water there is always growth. And where things grow there is always the possibility of fuel for the fire. Ashes, rubbish and dead organic material will become earth again, and the circle is complete: earth, metal, water, wood and fire.

Visible and invisible

You may be wondering what this has to do with feng shui. The answer is everything. The five elements are images of ingenious processes that are happening within us and in nature on a visible level and on an invisible level. The life force – chi – accommodates the five elements in yin and yang form. Chi is invisible, but it is working in us and around us.

We can see that something is burning when we light a candle or witness a house fire, but we do not literally see the fire in a person with a burning enthusiasm for something. Or the fire that is raging in a hyperactive person. We note the engagement and the restlessness but we don't see the fire element. We see the water in a spring and in lakes and rivers and we feel it on our bodies when we go for a swim or stand in the shower. But we do not see any physical sign of water when we are standing opposite someone who is terrified – we just see someone who is frightened. We recognise intelligence or intelligent solutions when we meet them, but we do not see the role of the water element. The elements express themselves in nature and also in humankind, and their relevance to buildings is particularly powerful.

In nature it is the season that decides which of the five elements is dominant at a particular time and what the consequences will be for the other four elements – and thus for all life. Fire, for instance, is the right element in summer when the sun is at its height and everything is fine and warm. But it has little strength in the middle of the winter. Nevertheless, all the elements are always present and all the functions are decisive for life on the planet.

As I've already mentioned, yin and yang and the five elements are central to Chinese medicine, both for diagnosis and for treatment. This knowledge, however, can also be used to analyse other aspects of human life, such as the amount of luck fate bestows upon us when we enter the world. Since time has varying characteristics, the actual moment of birth can inform us of the composition and strength of the five elements in the very first breath we draw. It may consist of the five elements in a balanced state or in an unbalanced state. One or more of the five elements may actually be missing. However that may be, this moment will mark us and its imprint will accompany us for the rest of our lives.

The five elements nourish, control and drain one another (more on this in Chapter 4). They are also called the five phases of life or the five life processes and, naturally and logically, they are closely connected to life energy. They are also strong expressions of time and space. Since they are cosmic in origin we talk of fast heaven energies as opposed to slow earth energies or stumbling man energies. They give life to everything, even to buildings created by man. They sometimes arrive in a house in a balanced form and create the most harmonious life situation for those who live there. Sometimes, unfortunately very often, the five elements end up in serious disharmony inside the four walls of the building. The most important cause of this is the heaven direction – how the architect has positioned the house on its plot or located the apartment. This, taken together with the temporal epoch we are in at a particular time, determines much of our earth luck in this world.

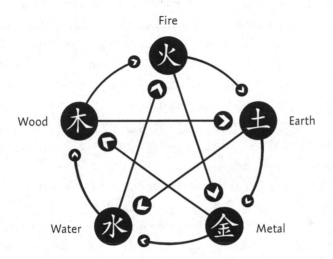

The five elements which the universe consists of according to traditional Chinese cosmogony are: earth, wood, metal, fire and water. These follow each other in an unending cycle and are linked to the heaven directions, seasons, colours, tones, the organs of the body, historical epochs and many other things. Together with yin and yang the five elements are part of a concept in which everything in the universe is joined in a cyclical process governed by cosmic principles.

The house and 'flying stars'

Each of the five elements is dominant in its own direction: fire in the south, water in the north, wood in the east, metal in the west, and the earth element has its place at the centre or 'in between' –

47

that is to say, in a sub-cardinal direction. The elements position themselves according to a fixed pattern within the four walls of a building depending on where it stands in relation to the heaven directions – the direction to which the face of the house is turned. And the converse: what does the compass needle show in the direction the house is 'sitting', and to which direction is it turning its back? The pattern of elements is, however, not fixed for all time. As we saw earlier, everything is in a constant state of change and consequently this pattern changes over time. We all know that pride comes before a fall and superpowers and great empires never last forever; flourishing towns and regions have had their struggles in the past and will also have their struggles in the future. Houses, too, have their splendid times and their not so splendid times. You only have to look around you or take a quick glance in the history books to recognise this.

Time is connected to the same qualities and characteristics that are linked with directions. At 12 noon the fire element (south) is dominant, whereas the water element (north) is characteristic of the midnight hour. Sunrise in the morning tells of a new day, a new start, which means that the morning is characterised by growth energy from the wood element (east). And sunset in its turn tells us that the day is waning; we withdraw and nature closes down. Evening is characterised by the metal element (west).

Similarly, spring – a new start – is the season of the wood element, summer that of fire, autumn that of metal and winter the season of water.

Long, long ago, however, brilliant minds worked out that there are even longer time spans that follow similar cycles. In these longer periods (see page 51) the five elements – the processes – follow their plan of action on an even larger scale. It is possible to calculate this and one important technique in feng shui sets about revealing how the five elements 'enter' and settle in every building, both large and small, at every point in time.

In order to reveal how the five elements affect a house (or apartment, shop or office block) we use what is called a flying star technique. Once again the starting point is an ancient observation of heaven and earth. The wise shamans discovered a pattern that has been named 'the seal of Saturn' which, in feng shui, is connected to numerical values that reveal how the five elements behave. Originally, colours rather than numbers were used to explain the different influences year by year and month by month: descriptions such as '2 yellow', '5 black', '4 jade green', and so on are still used even today and they tell of powerful time-determined or fate-determined influences. (The five elements are also linked with colours, but they express completely different qualities from those we are discussing here and they should not be confused; see Chapter 4.) All cultures have magic numerical patterns and human beings love numerology and number magic. There is a sense in which feng shui can be called a large numerical system, but it is only ostensibly so. The numbers and calculations in feng shui are not for their own sake or for magic purposes; rather they are aids to understanding the processes of nature. And like nature itself, feng shui is full of exceptions to every rule, every pattern and every system that is uncovered. This makes feng shui an even more fascinating subject to study.

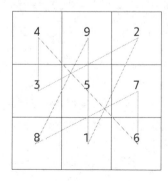
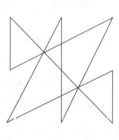

According to feng shui, the seal of Saturn is the pattern that comes closest to revealing the energy laws around us. The numbers that are used connect to the elements, to yin and yang, to the seasons, to the cycle of night and day and to the heaven directions. In other words, a powerful and practical calculator. And it has many, many layers, which an experienced feng shui expert knows by heart.

The numbers express directions, so what you are looking at here is also a map with all the cardinal and sub-cardinal directions. We can find the odd numbers in the cardinal directions: 1 north; 9 south; 3 east; 7 west. The even numbers indicate the sub-cardinal directions: 8 north-east; 4 south-east; 2 south-west; 6 north-west.

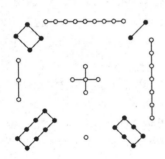

4	9	2
3	5	7
8	1	6

Lo shu: The pattern on the left was noticed on the shell of a tortoise over four thousand years ago and the sages interpreted it as an important universal pattern. In feng shui it is used in the flying star technique which discloses how the five elements distribute themselves in buildings constructed by mankind.

The flying star technique is used to reveal where the five elements are positioned in all the rooms in every house. The nine numbers relate to the five elements in the following way: 1=water; 2=earth; 3=wood; 4=wood; 5=earth; 6=metal; 7=metal; 8=earth; 9=fire.

Thus two of the numbers relate to the wood element, two to the metal element, no fewer than three to the earth element, whereas the water and fire elements only have one number each. Fire and water are fundamental elements for all life on the planet, and they are powerful. Fire and water give us life, but they also represent life-threatening and destructive forces.

Each of the directions and each of the numbers is thus connected to an element. In a house that is positioned with its front towards the south-east and its back to the north-west, for instance, the front middle inside the house will consequently be influenced by wood and the back middle by metal. Additionally, time energy will determine the other elemental influence in the house. A composite set of elements is located in every house.

Some houses are lucky and have good energies for well-being in the form of favourable combinations of elements in rooms in which the inhabitants can benefit from them. Other houses have accumulations of elements in conflict and this, of course, influences the people who live in the house, particularly when the conflicting energies are present in rooms in which the inhabitants spend a lot of time. Some of these combinations contribute to health problems, and the most serious of these elemental influences should be avoided in the bedrooms, in the kitchen or in the middle of the house (the 'tai chi', see Chapter 4). If they are situated in those places, we must either change our use of the room or find ways of curbing the influence.

We are dealing with powerful forces here and they can lift you triumphantly or trip you up and challenge you at every turn. Take the years we now have behind us: during the previous 'feng shui period' – that is, the 21 years from early 1996 to late 2016 – the world has been dominated by yang wood, which means start-up energy, getting going, new creations and inventions. That's true, isn't it? Just think of all the huge technological advances the world has seen time and again in recent years. Another characteristic of yang wood is noise and clamour. Could anything be more typical of the reality we live in? The world has become a noisy place and quiet is a rare luxury. The noise consists of the signals, warnings and communications related to the energy, which in the natural world is best heard as claps of thunder.

The pattern the five elements have followed in all buildings across the whole world during these years has led to critical accumulations of the earth element and contributed to exacerbating the following phenomena: digestive problems, obesity, conflicts, divorces and chaos. In addition to all that, there have been certain combinations of other elements connected with heart disease and cancer. Is all this familiar? The unfavourable accumulation of earth energy is invisible, but that does not mean it is any less urgent and challenging: it is earth energy that is quite unable to give life to anything at all. The good news is that we are on our way out of that period and entering a new period which will give houses and buildings completely new combinations of elements – with new challenges, of course, but also new possibilities.

To set about using the flying star technique to demonstrate what is happening in every single house lies beyond the scope of this book. As has already been mentioned, there are 16 different possibilities for how the five elements may be positioned, and the starting point is how the house is positioned in terms of direction and the feng shui period that is dominant. Even though we have entered a new period (2017–2044), the previous period will continue to influence our houses for some time to come. A competent practitioner of classical feng shui knows the best way of tackling this transition.

A brief summing-up

What lies at the heart of all the powerful, Eastern knowledge of acupuncture, qi gong, tai chi, meridian theory and, not least, feng shui is the recognition of a constant creative force expressed through five fundamental processes/five elements and the contrasts and reciprocity of yin and yang. According to Chinese holistic thinking, the same processes are at work in absolutely everything, in the enormous macrocosm – the universe – and in the microcosm that we on Earth are part of.

The five elements thus represent five different sides of the life force, five sorts of characteristics, five different types of 'stardust' if you like. They are connected both with the directions and with temporal cycles. Just think, for instance, of what characterises winter – the season we are best known for in Norway. It is cold and there is snow, both of which belong to the element water. The water element is dominant in the north. The summer is the opposite pole. It is warm, things germinate and flower and there is activity everywhere. Heat and sun definitely could not belong to anything but the fire element and that is the yang of the natural world. Fire belongs to the south. When the sun reaches its high point in the heavens, it is in the south, and that is the middle of the day.

You will remember that once the top is passed the process goes downwards, yang loses its power and allows yin to take over. The sun moves to the south-west and west and its heat and light decline, shadows grow longer with the approach of afternoon and evening. The element that takes over as the sun goes down is metal. But the earth element surfaces between fire and metal and it is an immensely important transitional element. As we shall see in Chapter 4, metal needs protection against intense heat. After all, we all know that fire melts metal.

SUPPORT IN LIFE

As I'm sure you know by now, feng shui is not interior design. Feng shui is concerned with all the factors that support or fail to support the physical building we live and work in. Those factors may be visible or they may be invisible. With the help of feng shui it is possible to make every building a safe, healthy and good place to be.

For good or bad, every aspect of human life is influenced to some extent by the address you have chosen to move to. Perhaps it is a posh address that is the most important thing to you and you have the means to make that choice. But life is not just about having a good address: your personal fate and energy system harmonises with the dwelling, not with the address. So there's the house with its walls, corners, entrances, windows, bends, extensions, projections and, last but not least, the structures around it. And along you come as the new owner, with a life that is changing according to what fate has in store for you. Feng shui has methods of analysis to reveal this and, once again, it is the five elements that come into play.

Let us say that everything has been going well for you, the buyer of the property: you have a good and secure job, a good income, a nice family and a good life. You and your family decide to move to a better district and the house at the good address seems to be the right choice. What you do not know, and what none of us know, is what awaits us round the next corner. You may perhaps be entering a phase in your personal cycle of fate (life, as we know, has its ups and downs) that will not nourish you and provide you with the same full and beneficial lucky fate as before. It may even have begun to turn against you rather. The choices you make are no longer the most favourable. Now we come to the part that is difficult for rational Western minds to comprehend:

the house into which you are moving will actually contribute to and exacerbate the very challenges that life is now throwing at you.

It sounds remarkable, and it is mysterious, so how do we go about unravelling this mystery? If you had all the answers, you would not be reading this book. But if you are one of the people who realises it's only human to acknowledge that we don't have all the answers and that mysteries actually spice up our spiritual development, then you are better placed to go along with the statement that a house is not just four walls and a roof. Whether the house is simple or grand, it will still be standing on a plot and wherever it is standing it will be uniquely subject to the influences of earth and heaven. We – the people in the middle – will don this 'overcoat' and when we move in the overcoat may feel as if it is tailor-made for us, or we may perhaps feel that it needs altering at once and so we set about making some changes, improvements and extensions.

In terms of energies, however, we turn out to be in harmony with the house. If the house could speak, it would be pleased to claim that it had attracted the right person or the right family. If you had heard it make such a claim, you would have protested and said that you were the one who had sought out and chosen the house. Both are right, but the house is the one with the stronger energy so, like it or not, you will just have to accept that something has happened that is outside your control.

From the top and downhill all the way
One of my clients was moving from one managerial position to another in a new company at about the same time as the poshest house in the district came on the market. He was earning a good salary, felt on top of things, was optimistic and ready for further success, both for himself and for the company. His wife had a

good secure job and they had two healthy children of school age. Where they were living was a bit small and the posh, spacious house with its address and its view was tempting.

They got the house – and everything in life took a turn for the worse, particularly for the husband. Suddenly, there were cut-backs at his new place of work and he was moved around and given a role in which he felt he was neither heard nor seen. He thought he would have been able to contribute much to get the company back on an even keel, but was not allowed to. He shared his thoughts with his colleagues but no one supported him. He was unable to get any peace in the new house. He started having sleep problems which, together with anxiety and stress, led to bad moods. His relationship with his children was affected by the changes and, of course, marital life suffered too. He became depressed, negative and lacking in energy.

This was the point at which I was contacted. There was nothing the matter with the husband's intuition because one of the first things he said to me was that there must be something totally wrong with the house. He had no real idea what feng shui was all about, but someone had recommended he get in contact with me. His wife told me later that they had wondered at first whether feng shui worked by driving out restless spirits and they were relieved to find that my approach to the house operated on a very different plane. Since I obviously cannot illustrate a client history with pictures, facts, place names and personal names, this example has been redacted, but it nevertheless sticks very close to reality. It covers all the ground necessary to explain what feng shui is and how it is possible to reveal connections between the house and the people who live in it.

This house is a perfect illustration of the challenges that can be caused by location and architecture. The first thing I noticed was all the obstacles between the front gate and the entrance door.

A steep set of steps up to the house was particularly decisive. We all know that it is more difficult to move upwards rather than across and down and in this case life energy was reaching the entrance in a pretty exhausted state. New energy enters primarily through the entrance door. This large house needed plenty to fill it, preferably fresh and vital energy that could fill all the rooms. But the great bulk of this house was lying there gasping for nourishment. The big, grand house had a poor supply of fresh energy. The entrance section was elegant and fine, but the door itself was set right back and actually difficult to see since it lay in shadow. It is never lucky when energy has to struggle to find its way.

Living in a house standing on high ground can cause problems, for where things go up they must also necessarily go down at some time or place. In this case, the ground went down steeply in two places – in the front (west) and in the south. The terrain on the north side had less of a slope because the garden was nicely terraced. The back had a slight feeling of being no-man's-land but, seen with feng shui eyes, the most important thing about it was that it was flat – that is to say, there was nothing in the terrain to support the house. An attempt at a hedge and a neighbouring house a short distance away were the only things. And the back was rather dark and dead, in addition to which it was a dump for unused slabs, stacks of planks, timber and bits of junk.

Houses need life-giving chi

Even before entering the house I had noted several factors that were bound to create challenges. A house that does not receive sufficient nourishment from its surroundings cannot provide nourishment and proper support for its inhabitants. A basic principle of feng shui is to ensure that a house receives a supply of life-giving chi in the best way possible – that is to say, neither too rapidly and violently nor too sluggishly and fussily.

And at the same time the building needs to be helped to retain the energy. It needs supportive structures at the back and on each side. Support for the back is not difficult to understand: you only need to remember how often you find something to lean on, put your back against or choose to sit with something supporting your back whenever you have the chance. The back of a house represents what we are turning our back on, the past, and the past is vitally important for the present and for what is to come. Like people, buildings need something to rest against and if they do not have it they lose energy, grow weak and are less able to take care of us. The rear of the house, therefore, also represents the health aspects of the inhabitants. When the support at the back is weak, we often find that health and illness are serious issues for the people who live in the house. Sometimes there may be a steep downhill slope behind the house, or it may be an unpleasant, dark and inaccessible area: situations like that are particularly challenging.

Heaven on earth
The ideal situation for a dwelling is to be surrounded by what feng shui calls 'the five heavenly animals'. This is a symbolic description for shapes in the surrounding area; a house located in such a position will create the optimal conditions for a good life. And which of us doesn't want as much as possible of heaven here on earth?

Support behind the house is represented by a tortoise. That honour has been bestowed upon the tortoise because it has a rock-hard shell which is very hard to crack. The tortoise is very slow-moving and its only way of protecting itself is by drawing the soft parts of its body into the shell. A house, which is supposed to take care of those who live in it, should provide that kind of safe and secure shell.

A protective 'tortoise' in the form of an elevation in the landscape, or perhaps another house, will offer support. In earlier times when people had greater freedom when it came to choosing their dwelling, people were at pains to find shelter from cold winds from the north, which is why a protective elevation or ridge behind the house is frequently to the north. This is why the tortoise is often referred to as blue or black (water element in the north; see Chapter 4).

The exact opposite to the rear or back of the house is, of course, the front: the face of the house. The front represents the future, our children and their future. Ideally speaking, this is where the phoenix should have a chance to spread its wings freely, and so we should find or create the best conditions for it to do so.

We want this area to be light and open. It is a cause for concern if there is a building cutting out the view in front of your house. Not just because the view is no longer so good, but also because the future is suddenly being blocked out. We do not want the future to be closed off, particularly not our children's future.

On the other hand, perhaps the view is fine and the phoenix wide open but the ground slopes steeply away as in the example I have been telling you about. That means that the life energy is not being sufficiently looked after: it is flowing away from the house and its people.

Traditional portrayals of the phoenix depict it as being red. In the ideal feng shui arrangement it is positioned facing south (the fire element which is primarily linked with the fiery red colour). To be able to enjoy the heat of the sun has always been just as important as finding protection from cold north winds, so the perfect position in traditional feng shui was to have the phoenix in the south. It is self-evident, however, that it is not possible to position all the millions of houses on the planet according to this ideal. But irrespective of which direction the building faces, whether it is a detached house, a terrace, a cabin, shed or apartment block, the surroundings are important. And what we need in front of the house is a good – that is to say, bright and open – phoenix.

Copyright © Komvell, Dreamstime.com

On one occasion early in my career as a feng shui consultant I was called to a young family that had moved into a terraced house on a large housing estate. All kinds of 'structures' within the family had suddenly been changed. Both parents were utterly worn out and the children fought and fussed and protested about absolutely everything. The mother of the family was so down that she wondered whether she was sickening for some illness, but consoled herself with the thought that it was all because of moving and changing to a new environment, new school, new teachers and so on. The front and entrance section of their terraced house was facing east, something that might have been thought good in itself. The problem, however, was that not a single ray of healthy new energy from the life-giving morning sun fell upon the happy face of the house because it was completely blocked out by a tall, looming block of flats. The children in the family discovered very quickly and keenly that their future had been shut out. The adults lost a sense of direction and purpose – after all, there was nothing to look across to. Everything in front of them was closed off and in shadow. An open phoenix means good support, but when it is closed off it contributes to problems of one sort or another. And it's worse for the next generation since they, after all, are the future.

In addition to all that, each side of a house needs strong, protective 'arms' that can ensure that the life energy is retained and enabled to do its job. A tiger and a dragon, respectively, have the honour of illustrating this.

We all need certain fundamental things to be in place for us to be able to live full-value lives. We need care and love and the opportunity for free and creative development, but simultaneously we need structure and responsibility and order, and we need a goal and purpose. As we are growing up, it is our parents who have the responsibility for providing all this, and in one way or another they represent yin and yang to us, safe care and responsible vigour. If the house has well-balanced and supportive structures on each side (a good balance between 'tiger' and 'dragon'), the mother and father in the family – woman and man, female and male characteristics and values – will be cared for in a balanced manner.

Copyright © Insima, Dreamstime.com

Strong harmony

When my client in the grand house stands at the front door every morning on his way to the office after yet another night of poor sleep, he is weary and, far from being in a good mood, he despairs at the thought of yet another meaningless day at work. Right in front of him he sees a steep set of steps going down to the garage and the front gate. He stands there, filled with heavy and depressing emotions and having black thoughts about the future. But he does not suspect that his own despair matches what the house is offering him – or, to be more accurate, what the house is not able to offer him.

To his left there is a steep slope down. The house is solidly built and has good supporting walls, but there is nothing to retain the energy on that side – the 'dragon' side. The dragon is supposed to be supportive of the man of the house and of all the traits that pertain to the male principle: rationality, responsibility, action, structure, focus, etc. The dragon is absent here. The slope falls away steeply, and it is a long way down.

The opposite side is the 'tiger' side. Since the ground falls away on this side too, the woman and the female aspects of existence are insufficiently cared for in terms of energy, but given the layout of the garden she, at least, is not critically exposed. This, in fact, matches the reality I have experienced in the family. The woman of the house is tired and worried because her husband is having such difficulty, but she herself is not directly afflicted.

The left hemisphere of the brain is the one that deals with logic and rational thought and we associate it with the characteristics we ascribe to the masculine principle. This hemisphere controls the right-hand side of the body, although the Chinese nevertheless stick firmly to the notion of the left side being associated with everything masculine. The right side of the body and the right hemisphere relate to everything that has to do with the feminine principle. Our eyes are located in our faces and thus at the front of the body; when we stand at the front of the house and look to the front, support for the male is to our left and support for the female to our right. If there is any support, that is.

The tiger is traditionally known as 'the white tiger' and white is the colour associated with the west (the metal element). The dragon is known as 'the green dragon' and green is associated with the east (the wood element). The tortoise is in the north, the phoenix in the south, the tiger in the west and the dragon in the east: this is a kind of ideal image which is only valid when the house is positioned so that its back is to the north.

Very, very many people live in houses which are positioned differently from this on the map and in the terrain. The back of the house may face east, south-east, west, south-west, north-west, north-east, south and even, of course, north. In all of these cases we are seeking support at the back and at the sides. At the back, irrespective of the direction, we need a protective tortoise. On the left-hand side as we stand looking out from the front of the house we need a supportive dragon and on the right-hand side a supportive tiger. (Note that the front of the house is not necessarily always where the entrance door is situated – the door may sometimes, for a variety of reasons, be at the side of the house or at the back.)

A good balance is the desired ideal. It should be open and free out in front of us, but the ground should not fall away. And there ought to be something that catches and holds the energy and allows the house to benefit from it – a border, fence, hedge or something capable of retaining the energy.

And what about indoors?

You are possibly wondering whether I bothered to consider the inside of the house at all. I did, of course, and there was no shortage of challenges there too: changes of level – steps between the storeys – caused disturbed and disrupted energy; large sheets of window glass created an atmosphere that was much too yang and consequently restless; many of the windows went from floor to ceiling without any sills or mouldings to prevent the energy flowing out; the positioning of the beds was less than ideal, and the adults had placed their double bed so that they were lying with their heads towards the window.

There was a great deal to be done and very much of it revolved around a lack of support and no possibility to achieve peace and relaxation, recovery and new strength. A house should not tire you out – quite the opposite, it should be a good and safe place to recharge your batteries.

As if it wasn't enough that the client completely lacked any support in the form of a dragon, there were even more problems caused by the position and architecture of the house. These had a critical influence on the family and, above all, on the life of the man of the house. There will be more about this in the next chapter.

2 WHY FENG SHUI?

When life has gone awry, it may be because of the house.
It may be that there are patterns that are repeating themselves,
perhaps things have come to a standstill, or are happening too suddenly.
Feng shui deals with change, feng shui is change
and feng shui creates change.

FENG SHUI ALWAYS MEANS CHANGE

So what is it that we really do, those of us who call ourselves feng shui advisers and claim that we are interested in people's lives, not their furniture or curtains?

The example given in the last chapter tells of great changes in the life of a family. Is it simply chance that the downturn in the man's situation began when they moved to the new house? If you believe that nothing is connected to anything else and reject the idea that there is a weave and pattern to life into which we are woven as well as being weavers, then it is quite natural to believe that everything occurs by chance. But what do we mean when we say by chance? What is chance? If instead of 'chance' we think of a jigsaw piece that we are putting into the jigsaw puzzle that is our life, we see that every 'chance' is part of a bigger picture. Everything connects with everything else.

Feng shui deals with completeness and with the connection between all things. But above all it deals with change and with understanding the nature of change. What happens in the wake of a change? How to create beneficial change? Life is changed because we do something in one area or another (man luck), because we extend or adapt our house or move to another house (earth luck), or because a factor connected to time energy (a new period in life or a special year) is decisive in some way (heaven luck). Changes can happen for better or for worse, and sometimes a counter-action is not merely desirable, but may be vital. But how can we know what the effect of a counter-action or intervention can or should be if we do not know what is going on?

Feng shui is change and feng shui creates change. There are times when we can achieve a great deal by arranging for better support or by removing blockages such as, for instance, an obvious physical barrier that shuts out a brighter future. And we can follow simple but important advice about creating flow (keep the entrance hall clear so that the house can breathe), move the dustbins away from the entrance area (to prevent the rubbish energy being drawn into the house), or improve the lighting in order to create a more active and life-enhancing atmosphere. But there is much, much more.

A feng shui expert uses his or her senses well and develops them to an extreme degree in order to be able to take in everything going on in the surroundings of a house. It is a drama that can only properly be seen and understood when seen through the lens of feng shui. And it's also necessary to dig down to the deeper layers of the surroundings and of the house itself in order to reveal more. It is beginning to be accepted that the human body has a measurable layer of aura. The house with which we surround ourselves is yet another layer of energy, and these energies are measureable. The feng shui compass is nothing short of an x-ray machine!

Energy doctor

Just as a doctor has a stethoscope, the energy detective can rely on an advanced tool, the energy compass. It's no exaggeration to say that it's a surgical instrument. The compass – lo pan – captures all the available information about the invisible energy influences in the 360° around us. The eight trigrams and 64 hexagrams of the I Ching (the book of the nature of change) provide the basis for the construction of the compass. The hexagrams contain all the information about everything around us (and in us) and they could be called the DNA of the universe. On the feng shui compass each hexagram – also known as a 'kwa' – covers 5.625°. And each of these directions is dominated in unique ways by five fundamental or universal energies and can be translated to the following recognisable categories in human life: myself and my peers; what I create; what I control; what controls me; my resources. Thus the energies also tell us about children, partner, friends, parents, health, economy, position and status, competitors.

Everything that lives on Earth has a biological urge to ensure the survival of its species. We produce progeny to the best of our ability. As I see it, falling in love, cannot be anything other than yin and yang working all out to ensure we have the right biological and genetic match to produce the best possible starting point for our progeny! When we fall in love, we easily become 'psychotic' and disengage reason and thought, as indeed we have to if the choice of partner is to be made on the basis of premises we cannot control with our heads. Welcome to the world of energies!

People do not only create children; they also create careers, they are creative and they work. If you desire to make changes to your career or if you are yearning for greater creative development, measurements with the feng shui compass can provide much information about the possibilities available in the house you inhabit or in your office, study or studio. There are parts of the house where it is easier to study and concentrate than elsewhere in the house: reorganising the house to achieve better space for studying and improved exam results has to be better than resorting to performance-enhancing drugs, which are common not only in the sporting world but also among students.

Couples who want children but fail to conceive can be helped by the same type of measurements: is child energy present in the room in which you are trying to reproduce? It may be present, but perhaps the positioning of the bed is not catching the energy. By using the feng shui compass it will be possible to locate the energy and arrange the room accordingly. Even though this may not provide an answer or be the solution for everyone, it can offer a good alternative to time-consuming and expensive IVF attempts.

Since the compass and the hexagrams contain such detailed knowledge about all aspects of life, feng shui in the hands of an expert can contribute to a better existence and provide more and better possibilities for most people. Is your shop not going well? One reason might be that money energy is not reaching the door in proper quantities, or the till is not positioned where it should be. An unsatisfactory home life will hardly be improved if there are quarrelsome energies constantly intruding in the house.

Universal patterns

Each of the 64 hexagrams, which lie in a fan shape around us, consists of two trigrams. In other words, the six lines in a hexagram consist of two kinds of universal basic energy. One basic energy, a trigram, thus consists of three lines, and there are eight of them. As has already been noted, the eight trigrams are expressions of everything that exists. Everything in existence – from the climate and natural world to the directions, the seasons of the year, human characteristics and behaviour, occult phenomena, the body and its organs – can be classified with the help of the trigrams. The trigrams are profound symbols and the three lines that make them up represent heaven and earth, with mankind as the middle line between them.

Long, long ago, by using this code system, a language was provided for both comprehensible and incomprehensible phenomena. The three lines are either whole or broken, and they represent yang (whole line) and yin (broken line). There are eight possible ways in which three yin and yang lines may be combined.

Heaven	Earth	Thunder	Wind	Fire	Water	Lake	Mountain

The eight trigrams are named after natural phenomena: heaven and earth, thunder and wind, fire and water, lake and mountain. Each trigram is also connected to one of the stars in the Plough since, according to the shamans and sages of ancient China, Planet Earth is a microcosm that mirrors the great macrocosm in the enormity of space around us. As was described in the previous chapter, this knowledge is used in measuring and revealing what kind of energy influences there are to be found in a house or on a plot.

The trigrams tell us about nature and life in movement. They have light, dark, sound and rhythm in them – yin and yang. They are explained by means of two sequences, one of which is like a universal and divine illustration of the original, ideal, completely balanced state. This sequence is called 'early heaven' and expresses the universal energy around us. It can also be viewed as an extension of the harmony that the actual yin-yang symbol illustrates – total balance, but without life – a virtually perfect still image:

The early heaven sequence shows that heaven is above us: the trigram with the three lines is at the top and that is also where the light part of the yin-yang symbol – the sun – is at its widest in the illustration. The sun (the fire trigram) is there, rising in the east with the moon (the water trigram) positioned opposite in the west. The trigrams, the energies, the phenomena are positioned in pairs immediately above each other. Heaven and earth are in balance (south and north), fire and water are under control (east and west), thunder and wind are linked (north-east and south-west), mountain and lake (north-west and south-east) are there as a beautiful illustration of reality. 'Early heaven' is like an image of an eternally valid truth.

It expresses a balanced state, but that does not make it unimportant. Very few feng shui approaches use the early heaven sequence in their calculations and analyses, not because it is difficult to understand but because it was vital in earlier times to conceal precisely how effective it is. The cryptic texts are inexplicable (upside down and back to front) and most people have given up trying to understand them. Fortunately, however, not everyone has, and there are still classical feng shui masters who understand this knowledge. Classical feng shui in the form practised in Chue Style feng shui taught by Grand Master Chan Kun Wah combines early and later heaven in an advanced form of feng shui practice with very powerful results.

Change is already a fact in the later heaven sequence. The dance of yin and yang has started and with it an eternal process of change and development. In this we see how everything has come to life and is where it is meant to be when nature takes its course:

SE	S	SW
Eldest daughter (Wind)	Middle daughter (Fire)	Mother (Earth)
Hips, hair, gall bladder	Heart, small intestine, eyes	Stomach, womb
☴	☲	☷
E		W
Eldest son (Thunder)		Youngest daughter (Lake)
Feet, legs, liver		Mouth, lungs
☳		☱
NE	N	NW
Youngest son (Mountain)	Middle son (Water)	Father (Heaven)
Hands, arms, spleen	Kidneys, bladder, ears	Head, lungs
☶	☵	☰

The sun (fire) moves across heaven: all life starts in the east in the morning (wood energy) and subsides in the west (the metal energy of evening); the moon (water) in the north in the night sky stands right opposite the sun in the south. The sub-cardinal directions represent transitions in which, when needed, the important earth energy fulfils a buffer role as go-between.

A feng shui family

In feng shui the eight trigrams are also called a family. The feng shui family has a mother, a father and six children – three daughters and three sons (see the illustration above.) As we have noted, these trigrams express all sides of existence and, as in the illustration, this is how they are placed in every building. When they are found intact around us in a dwelling, it means that all aspects are alive and, in terms of energies, the process of being human is being taken care of. It does not mean that we should all have three sons and three daughters: we may live alone or we may have ten children or two children or no children. The fact that the trigrams are represented in our dwelling means that in energy terms we are surrounding ourselves with everything these trigrams represent. If not all of them are represented, perhaps because the house has a fancy design and lacks one or more corners of the complete energy square that is desirable, or perhaps because it is an apartment squeezed in with many other units in an apartment block (with a ground plan virtually identical to a pistol), the developer's lack of planning presents us with challenges. So everyone involved with the design and development of dwelling places is welcome to join a course!

If a house lacks a section – a corner, large or small – it means that the actual trigram and all it stands for will not be represented.

Which of the energies is excluded depends on how the house is positioned in terms of direction. The missing corner may be located in any one of the eight directions.

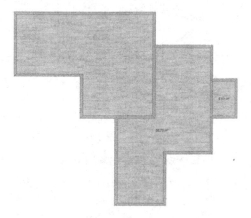

If the above apartment is positioned in the same way as the illustration on page 73, that is to say with the south at the top of the drawing and the north at the bottom, the following family members, body parts and health issues will be more or less endangered: south-west – mother, stomach, care; north-west – father, head, lungs, responsibility; north – second son, kidneys, hearing, flexibility; north-east – third son, arms, hands, spleen, inner peace; east – first son, legs, feet, liver, starting energy. Another apartment block in the same area and with the same type of apartments but facing a different heaven direction will, of course, have the same corners missing from the complete square, but different trigrams will be affected.

Cosmic DNA

Half of the trigrams are yin (mother and three daughters) and the other half are yang (father and three sons). The yin energy is expressed by a broken line, yang by a whole line. In other words, the trigram that consists of three whole lines is a completely yang trigram and simultaneously an image of energy in constant movement.

The trigram is called Heaven and it symbolises leader energy, responsibility and strength. Heaven energy is brisk and can have a merciless impact. We are subject to it and to the warm and life-giving sun, which is the most yang that exists in our universes. This trigram represents father in the feng shui family. The trigram stands for the masculine and penetrating, for strength, leadership and responsibility.

The trigram with the three broken lines is a completely yin trigram and an image of Mother Earth – an open, receptive and also stable energy. The trigram is called Earth and, just like mother, it can contain and bear everything. Mother Earth never lets us down and gives support and nourishment to everything that lives and germinates and grows. The trigram shows openness, receptiveness and the gift of fruitfulness. It is also the case that, energetically speaking, sons take most of their genetic material from their mother whereas daughters take most from their father. One can therefore recognise a daughter trigram because it consists of two whole lines and one broken, whereas the trigrams that represent sons have two broken lines and one whole one.

Thus it is one line in the trigram that informs us about gender – that is, whether it is a yin or yang trigram. When only one of the three is a broken line it means yin (daughter), whereas one yang line means yang (son). The placing of that one line – broken or whole – within the trigram tells us which daughter or son is being referred to. We have three lines and we start at the bottom of the trigram when we are to decide whether it is the first, second or third son or daughter. First come first: the bottom line represents the first son/daughter, the second line son/daughter number two, and the third line son/daughter number three. If you have four sons, the first line also represents the fourth: in other words, son/daughter number four also has the energy traits valid for son/daughter number one.

You are childless? Don't despair, for the trigrams also deal with all the other aspects of being a human being on this earth.

All eight trigrams are connected to the directions, the seasons and, it goes without saying, the five elements. Each trigram is characterised by an element and since there are eight trigrams and five elements there must be a pattern manifesting itself, preferably a logical and comprehensible pattern.

The four cardinal directions correspond to four of the five elements in pure form – as we have seen earlier. The logic is that where heat and fire are located – in the south – that is where the trigram called Fire is. In the north where it is cold and wet, that is where the trigram called Water is. In the east we find the trigram Thunder and in the west the metal trigram Lake. Wind lies in the south-east between Thunder and Fire, and Mountain is in the north-east between Water and Thunder.

When you are working with feng shui for a client, or in your own life for that matter, this is important knowledge because all the eight directions have different characteristics. Energy from the north-east is different to energy from the south or from the north-west, and so on. But it is also important to recognise all the other aspects and layers in the eight trigrams.

In addition to a trigram having a powerful connection with one of the family members in terms of energy, it also has all these other qualities and characteristics that are directly linked to the body, health and other aspects of being human (see the table below).

☳	East **wood**	first/eldest son (Thunder)	legs, feet	liver	start energy anger
☴	South-east **wood**	first/eldest daughter (Wind)	hips, thighs	gall bladder	quiet strength anger
☵	North **water**	second/middle son (Water)	ears, hearing	kidneys	flexibility fear
☲	South **fire**	second/middle daughter (Fire)	eyes, sight	heart, small intestine	openness hysteria
☶	North-east **earth**	third/youngest son (Mountain)	arms, hands	spleen, rectum	inner peace obstinacy
☱	West **metal**	third/middle daughter (Lake)	mouth	lungs	joy sorrow
☰	North-west **metal**	father (Heaven)	head	lungs	leadership authority
☷	South-west **earth**	mother (Earth)	belly	womb	care worry

If the building – your house or your flat – is designed in such a way that it forms a complete rectangle, square or otherwise, with none of the corners missing, it means that all eight of the trigrams are in place. The house is looking after the energy of all members of the family.

A house that has corners missing to the south-east and the south-west, for instance, will lack energy for the mother and the eldest daughter because of the absence of those trigrams. These are two trigrams that stand for very much that pertains to female characteristics and values: in the south-west it's a case of stomach, womb, earthing (earth), care and motherliness; in the south-east the gall bladder, hips, the small of the back, thighs, communication (wind), humility and female endurance and strength. In a house like this there is a strong probability that something connected with one or more of these aspects will become a challenging issue.

The solution, however, is neither given nor necessarily obvious and the effects on one family will be different from those on another. But a missing corner/trigram always gives rise to some vulnerability, and the more exposed to unfavourable influences the area is, the more serious the consequences may be. The opposite is the case when the trigram is well cared for. If it is lying in an extremely favourable direction and influenced by wonderful surroundings and influences, and if all of the rooms are being used exactly as they should be, life possibilities for the inhabitants of the house will turn up more frequently and more obviously. There will be a greater probability of good luck, success and a beneficial flow, or for good health, well-being and a harmonious domestic life.

The house always tells a story

It is sometimes difficult to determine which is the front and which the back of a house. In the case of apartments it is usually easy – look for the wall with the most windows and this is almost always the front. The back, which always has to be taken into account when considering support and health, and which also provides the starting point for many of the methods of feng shui, is located in exactly the opposite direction. If most of the windows in the apartment face south-west, its back will then be facing north-east, and so on.

With houses, the situation is rather more complicated. There are many factors involved and, as mentioned earlier, the front of a house is not necessarily where the entrance door is. The most decisive factor is how the house receives life energy. Something might look as if it is the front (windows=eyes, open, a view) but, for example, if this part of the house faces a garden with a fence or hedge round it without any possibility of access, it is probably not the front. It is often obvious which is the front and which the back, but just as often it can be a demanding procedure to decide which is which. For an experienced feng shui consultant, the answer usually falls into place after walking round the house a few times, but not always. Extensions and conversions can sometimes be confusing, not only for someone trying to assess the house but also for life energy, the chi. What is what in this place? Which is the way in? Is it actually possible to get in?

In a country like Norway yet another factor comes into play – the climate and the seasons. In winter we shovel a clear path to the entrance door, often at the back of the house, and lead people and chi in as best we can. In summer we open the terrace door wide and may even ignore the entrance door completely. The chi then has to put up with being led in along a different – and not always obvious – route across the lawn.

There are some houses where it is so difficult to decide on which is the front and which the back that the consultant has to take double measurements: east, for instance, seems in most ways to be the back, but there are also significant factors that suggest the north – not least the fine outlook towards the south, where there is also open space in front of the house. And so on. There are also situations involving extensions and other changes in which so much is happening, both with the house and with the family, that the house itself cannot decide for the moment. In this case the uncertainty and confusion will also leave its mark on the inhabitants. They, perhaps, find themselves in a life situation that is confused, or they are faced with major choices about which they cannot agree and come to a decision. Should we do this or should we do that? Move? Renovate from top to bottom? Rent out? Build an extension? The house is part and parcel of all this uncertainty, which leaves the feng shui consultant scratching his head.

Measurements taken from both possible directions – there are rarely more – to decide on back and front mean that it is possible to compare the results of the calculations with the reality of the family in the house, and at some stage in the process the feng shui consultant will come up with the right answer.

Another method of checking, and one which often provides a clear answer, is to look at the support on the tiger and on the dragon side. In order to do this it is necessary to have some knowledge of the inhabitants, which is why this method is particularly suitable for anyone uncertain about the front and back of their own house. Are the female and male aspects equally well looked after at your own home? Are you equals? Do you both feel well cared for? Is everything going well for both of you? Or are there noticeable differences? If there is a good balance between the supportive structures on each side, it is likely that there will be a balanced relationship between wife and husband, as long as other factors such as personal feng shui/fate are not involved. Is the woman of the house the stronger party? Is she busy, earning good money, holding down a good job – a top job even? Is she successful and doing well in many ways? She likes the house and she was perhaps the one who chose it? In this case it is not very likely that the house has a weak tiger side. The tiger side is to the right when you are standing in front of the house looking outwards; the dragon side is to the left. Does the ground slope down on one side, whereas the other side is higher and more vigorous? Is one of the partners struggling with health, work situation, dependency and so on? If so, it is highly likely that this can be traced back to lack of support.

If it is still unclear as to which is the front and which the back, we can fall back on 'spiritual feng shui' and put the question to the divination oracle I Ching.

The trigram in my life

Many solitary and divorced people think about taking a new companion. Will I find a new partner? Will I meet the man/woman of my life? Will I remarry?

I have had very many feng shui consultations with lone women in which these thoughts have been voiced. They are glad they have divorced and now they are wondering whether feng shui can explain why love is so long in coming. Often it's quite obvious: it is all about energy. When these women, happy to be free, acquire somewhere new to live, they are unconsciously attracted to a home that lacks a north-west corner – that is the trigram for father or man of the house. (After all, what do we know about feng shui and trigrams in our part of the world?) A man definitely has no part to play in her new life, so he is not present in the floor plan – not present in terms of the basic supportive energy, the trigram. There was a time when she found this a relief and a pleasure, as we can clearly see from the symbolism around her apartment: she has fine pictures hanging on her walls, particularly of women, often of just one woman; the woman figure is often slightly turned away, her face completely or partially concealed. The same symbolism is visible in other decorative objects – female figures, goddesses, angels, and always alone. Everything around this solitary woman is confirmation of the fact that there is no room for a man in her life. We get what we ask for, as the saying goes.

The walls with which we surround ourselves function as vision boards and we should pay attention to the powerful symbolism we put up around us. If we wish to become a twosome and have a love life with a partner, it would be a good idea to demonstrate this in various ways in our home. We might, for instance, hang up romantic pictures of couples, acquire a double bed and put a bedside table on each side of it.

I have often noticed how powerful an influence the absence of a north-east corner can have on the people in the house. North-east is governed by the energy of the trigram Mountain – youngest son. This is an energy that has to do with stability (the mountain) and finding peace and seeking inwards. If the house cannot contribute this, it may be difficult for some people – not everyone – to relax properly. When an individual's personal combination of energies offers the same type of challenge, I have often noticed that there is a great probability of the 'external layers of energy' appearing in his or her life drama, and the individual in question either lives or ends up in a residence with an incomplete north-east. (For the personal combination of energies see the eight signs in the Chinese horoscope in Chapter 4.) It seems as if they have a motor in their lives that is carrying them in the direction of burn-out. When many energy conditions or factors in life have the same content – or lack of such content – things move inexorably in that direction. Whether we call it fate or circumstance, there can be no doubt there is a pattern present.

But note this and note it well! A missing area, and consequently a missing trigram, does not mean that that is the end of it and it's time for you to move on the grounds that if you stay put the house is going to cause problems for your liver or your lungs or your head. Existence is much more nuanced than that. I have had consultations where several trigrams have been absent from a house and I have been unable to find any negative connections. I have seen how individual this is, and that's what makes it so attractive and interesting.

Some years ago, at about the time I was seriously becoming involved in my feng shui education, we decided to sell our house and move into an apartment. The purchase went through quickly on the basis of a prospectus that looked both practical and convenient and we acquired an excellent apartment with a fine view. We hardly had time to look at the plan, nor did we have any idea of the exact directions. When we moved in a couple of years later I discovered that the apartment completely lacked a north-west area. I had taken my feng shui exam earlier that year and I naturally felt that I should have avoided ending up in a situation like that. Anyway, I decided not to worry about the man of the house or anything else to do with that trigram: worrying gets us nowhere, as we all know. But that did not stop me keeping my eyes open and assessing things as we went along. What did I see? The man, in this case the man I live with – who has strong and well-balanced personal feng shui (the eight signs) – is still getting on extremely well after almost seven years in the apartment. The way we live is that we spend as much time as we can at a house in the country and during the working week he is busy with his job and has evening activities several times a week. In this case, then, there is harmony between the absent trigram and reality – the man of the house not being at home a great deal. So the absent trigram does not have any dramatic effect.

All the pieces of the puzzle

Back now (at last!) to the example of the family that moved into a fine house with a panoramic view at an upmarket address, in which, however, the father was depressed and listless. The house was architect-designed and individual, and it lacked several corners. Two directions/trigrams were completely missing – the whole of the north-west and virtually the whole of the south-west: both father and mother, then. The father was the one with the most obvious and acute problems, but the mother was struggling too: she was beside herself with worry about her husband. As you will recall, the house had a good tiger side, but absolutely no dragon side. On the dragon side the ground fell away steeply, whereas the tiger side had a terraced and well-worked garden.

There was, however, another part of the house I noted as being critical with regard to the lack of retention of energy and that was the west-facing area at the middle of the front. This was where the entrance section lay and, as we have seen, that is of major importance to the kind of energy the house is supplied with. The trigram for daughter number three lies in the west and there were only two daughters in this family so, at present, there was no member of the family who could be directly affected by the absence. But, additionally, this west trigram, the metal trigram which is also called Lake, represents mouth, joy, laughter and communication. It is through our mouths that we take in nourishment. The entrance door was set back so that there was a large hollow space, which meant that the trigram was partially absent from the body of the house, and the area was dark and silent. You will also remember that the ground fell away steeply in front of the house: so there were challenges here.

There was a similar challenge in the east, at the back of the house, where an even larger piece was missing. In the eastern sector of a house it is the energy for the first son that is being cared for, always assuming that the house is 'complete', which it was not in this case. The trigram belongs to the element of wood, which deals with the energy to get started, with the ability and will to get things moving, with activity and initiative.

This is a good point at which to mention an important question that should always be asked before you put in an offer or sign the contract: what has happened in this house in the past? Is it possible to discover anything about the history of the place and, if so, how should that information be interpreted?

The answer in this case was that the house was built by a prosperous businessman who went bankrupt just one year after moving in with his family. Most people will be sad to hear something of that sort, but they might also think it's a bonus because the house is on the market and they really, really want it. What they ought to be thinking is that they should stay well away from the place unless they want the same kind of thing to happen to them. The point is that when great changes take place in people's lives, the house and the plot it stands on are always contributors to those changes. When, for instance, the previous owners of an apartment have divorced, there will always be the probability that marital problems will arise in the lives of the next owners. Many people believe that people's problems and conflicts remain behind and 'infect' the next family and that the smart thing to do is to scrub away all the old memories before moving in. But when a pattern repeats itself from owner to owner, there are clearly greater forces at play and we find we are dealing with structural things, with trigrams, hexagrams, the influence of elements, the positioning of doors, the distribution of spaces, support and flow.

In this house it is the husband and father whose energy is being sapped. He feels he is being pressed down and held back, he finds it impossible to relax, and he no longer finds any joy in life. The house explains much of this, but there are other forces that affect people's lives too. Sometimes these things all coincide and become immensely challenging and almost insuperable.

To make the picture more complete, let me add a few more pieces to the puzzle. My client was so affected by the situation at home and at work that he was at risk of some kind of serious breakdown or illness at any moment. The house was unsupported on all sides and there was no support or rest indoors because, for instance, the window surfaces were far too large and the areas of supporting walls where one could lean back and relax were far too small. We have already noted that he felt no support for his own ideas and initiatives at work, that he was feeling very out of sorts, increasingly depressed and had stated that he would not be able to cope much longer. What are the other pieces that might fill out the picture and explain why a strong, secure and successful person found his life changed so completely?

No distinction is made in authentic classical feng shui between the place of residence and the people who live in it. We all have our personal feng shui, which is to say that we all have our own special make-up in energy terms, and this energy constitution is determined at the moment of birth. In Chinese astrology and in personal feng shui analysis, by using the five elements as the tools of analysis, it is possible to describe your constitution on the basis of the time you were born. Since feng shui treats both space and time, it must be possible to analyse time just as we analyse houses and rooms. This question was posited many thousands of years ago and the answer is ancient and well tested: time and space are in a constant process of change and follow the same kind of cyclical patterns. Every minute, every hour, day, month and year have a distinct character in terms of energy, which is why the moment of birth can tell us so much.

EIGHT SIGNS

The moment of birth consists of four important factors of different strength and power: the year, the month, the day and the time of day. Most people have heard of Chinese animal signs and probably know which animal of the Chinese zodiac relates to the year in which they were born.

Chinese astrology differs from Western astrology in most respects, and what is immediately apparent is that it is the year of birth rather than the month that is referred to. In Western astrology, if you are born between 22 May and 22 June you 'are' a

Gemini; in Chinese astrology you 'are' the sign that governs the whole year in which you are born – you might be a Horse, an Ox, a Rabbit or a Rooster. The Chinese zodiac has 12 animal signs, each of which has one year, and once the cycle of 12 is complete it starts again: Rat, Ox, Tiger, Rabbit, Dragon, Snake, Horse, Sheep, Monkey, Rooster, Dog and Pig.

But there is more to it than that. The 12 months of the year are also governed by one of the 12 animal signs and in this cycle the animals retain a fixed place from one year to the next. The Ox goes with January, the Tiger with February and so on. The 12 animals or energies have characteristics that connect them with the five elements. And, as we mentioned earlier, we can find the five elements in the seasons of the year.

The element wood, which belongs to spring, is thus the element that is connected to the months of spring and, in Chinese astrology, the spring months are the tiger month and the rabbit month, that is, February and March. The element fire belongs to summer and this is where we find the snake month and the horse month – May and June. Autumn, the season of metal, has the monkey month of August and the rooster month of September. And finally there is the water element with winter as its season: November is the pig month and December is called the rat month.

Four elements and eight animals, two of each element, one yin and one yang. The fifth element, earth, has the ability to act as a buffer and ensure good transitions, which is precisely what characterises the four 'intermediate months', January, April, August, October. Mother Earth's own element is represented by four reliable and powerful animals: the ox (January), the dragon (April), the goat (July) and the dog (October).

The days and hours are divided up according to the same system. The 12 animal signs follow one another day by day and after 12 days the cycle begins again. The same is true of the hours – with a minor exception: there are only 12 animal signs in the course of the 24 hours which means that each animal sign has to cover or govern two hours of the clock. We are now almost at the point where we can define the eight signs.

But why eight signs when we have been talking about four units: (1) year, (2) month, (3) day, (4) hour? The picture is more nuanced and existence more complicated.

Along with the (earthly) animal sign there is also a heaven influence which is expressed as one of the five elements in yin or yang form. Let us say we have a Year of the Horse. The horse is a fire sign and the horse is yang. An animal sign is also called an earthly branch and the time aspect can never be fully defined with the help of earth energy alone. It only tells half of the story.

Our globe rotates and follows its cosmic orbit and is never uninfluenced by the forces around it. The earth branch is therefore accompanied by a cosmic influence, by a heavenly stem, and in the case of the horse it has to be a yang heavenly stem because the horse is yang. In other words, the heavenly stem is an element influence which is either in yin or yang form.

And we have five elements, which means we have ten to choose from: yin and yang wood, yin and yang fire, yin and yang earth, yin and yang metal and yin and yang water. 2014, for instance, was a Year of the Horse (yang/fire) which was subject to a powerful heavenly influence from the element wood in yang form. Since wood feeds fire the fire energy was strong in 2014. The horse is the most yang of all the animal signs and it represents speed and action. 2014 was an eventful year in many ways.

Yang is followed by yin, after which yang returns, followed once more by yin, and so the cycle continues eternally. For example, 2015 was the Year of the Sheep, since the sheep follows the horse in the animal sequence. The horse is yang, followed by the sheep which is a yin earthly branch. It thus stands together with a yin heavenly stem. The sheep is earth and the heavenly stem in 2015 was wood, so that year we were dealing with a 'wood sheep'. What affects this sheep is that its energy, the earth energy or earth element, is controlled by the wood element, the heavenly stem. Control from above. Another word for control is collision.

Heaven energies are fast-moving energies and not always easy for us humans to predict and control. This became a clear pattern all around the world for the whole of the year 2015. Feng shui masters use advanced methods in order to predict how each year will turn out.

We will leave that particular theme at this point and return to our example. My point is to show that since every animal symbol (earthly chi) always occurs together with another sign (heavenly chi), the year, the month, the day and the hour will respectively be expressed by two symbols and consequently every birth time can be described with eight signs altogether. Here is a randomly chosen date and hour and quite probably the precise birth time for many new citizens of the world:

hour	day	month	year
壬	癸	辛	丙
yang water	yin water	yin metal	yang fire
戌	丑	卯	申
Dog, yang earth	Oxen, yin earth	Rabbit, yin wood	Ape, yang metal

The eight signs for someone born on 1 April 2016 between 20.00 and 22.00 (Summer Time, so actually between 19.00 and 21.00).

We are all born at a particular hour of a particular day and month and year. Thanks to the ancient shamans' decoding of energy at every point in time, the Chinese even today can tell the strengths and weaknesses of every point in time. Energy will change with the clock over the course of the day, showing a very different energy in the morning (wood energy) than in the middle of the day (fire) and the evening (metal energy). The time of birth, however, cannot be changed and it follows the individual as an energy imprint throughout life.

In the example given above, all five elements are in place at the time of birth. The day itself is a 'water day'. The eight signs are an energy imprint that will accompany us through our lives.

One of the signs represents the person him/herself and the analysis also includes individual periods of fate and influences from both years and months through life. It can tell us about health problems, career possibilities, economic challenges, happy surprises and the chances of getting married and having children. And much more.

The Chinese are fascinated by luck and chance and the focus is frequently on whether we are in a generally good period that could lead to good luck or whether it would be better to keep our heads down and not take too big a risk. It is not possible to reveal any of this by simply considering the year in which you were born. It is possible to have your fortune told on the street in Hong Kong and be told many remarkable truths based only on the year of your birth. But you should bear in mind that the fortune-teller is an expert when it comes to reading faces, body language and hands and has many good techniques to tell quickly who you are.

Fate

My client's eight signs told of strengths and possible challenges, as all birth horoscopes do. It revealed a strong disposition for business, but there were certain imbalances and vulnerabilities, none of them being any sort of extreme challenges, however. From these eight signs it is possible to produce an extended analysis of an individual's life from childhood to old age. Those of us who have lived a while know only too well that life has its ups and downs and that an up stage has a tendency to be followed by a down stage. How and where we encounter reverses or have luck on our side is an individual matter, but it can be read to a great extent in a personal element analysis.

Our man had had most things going for him for over 30 years. The element influences had supported him well for long periods. His life had unfolded as he had wished and most things went his way. But then things began to turn against him and for someone who is accustomed to a good flow it is difficult to taste defeat and to know how to tackle it. When he reached the age of 34 he entered a period of 15 years with, from the astrological perspective, an overdose of the element he needed least in life. Challenges lined up one after another and he experienced reverses and failures.

It was about halfway through this period when the house came on the market. This businessman and risk-taker had already suffered financial loss and difficulty but, naturally enough, he did not suspect he was in the middle of a cycle of fate during which his chances of success were small. So he went ahead and bought this grand, expensive house which, as it turned out, faced him with one challenge after another from day one onwards. It proved to be a 100 per cent match with his personal cycle of fate.

I have seldom had a more attentive client. His questions were answered at our first meeting and that was enough to restore his faith in life and its possibilities. The family immediately set about making changes to the house and the husband was given specific advice on how to use the five elements to strengthen himself and to relieve the pressure. After six months he decided to accept a job in a neighbouring town and they sold up and moved. In that process they were, of course, given feng shui help.

3 WHAT KIND OF FENG SHUI?

What about these short cuts and simple solutions then?
How profound are the changes achieved with simplified magic likely to be?
And how lasting will they be?

FROM SCIENCE TO OVER-SIMPLIFICATION

The most important reason for me taking up the serious study of feng shui was my growing frustration with all the peculiar things I encountered under the name of feng shui. After translating two feng shui books, reading a dozen others and attending various weekend courses, I had a strong feeling that there was something quite crazy about the claims being made in popular presentations. I had to make a decision: either that was the end of the whole business as far as I was concerned or I had to take up feng shui seriously. I did the latter, of course, because I sensed that there must be truth and understanding somewhere and that real feng shui was concerned with very different things to those I had been involved with so far.

There is truth in the saying that when the pupil is ready a teacher will appear. I found my teacher of authentic classical feng shui and I realised that my intuition had been right when, in spite of everything, I had decided to listen to my frustrated soul and started searching rather than slamming the door on the whole business.

When feng shui was introduced to the West, it was not as a scientific system dealing with how the forces of nature and universal life energy impact on buildings and how, in their turn, buildings shape those in them. It did not deal with an understanding of landforms and the laws of energy, or with favourable and unfavourable forms of influence, or with the wisdom passed down and refined for millennia, or with the connection between directions, cosmic influences and the effects of energy both around and within the house. It did not deal with profound insights into 'wind and water' and how we can benefit from the good and nourishing forces in our surroundings and avoid the negative forces. There was none of that! What was introduced instead was an instant pot-pourri in which the ingredients consisted of all kinds of exotic items from pure and simple superstition via powerful symbolism to number magic that promised to bring good luck. No wonder people were attracted. And who is to say that superstition does not sometimes have a grain of truth, that symbolism is devoid of meaning, or that magic cannot bring good luck? It was easy to take the bait.

It was easy, too, to call yourself Master, and many Western variants of feng shui were cobbled together with fancy names. There was American feng shui, and Indian-American feng shui, and Tibetan-American feng shui, but were any of them feng shui? Hocus-pocus theories even arose in Asia: ancient wisdom had become fashionable there just as it had here, and in recent times easily marketable concepts of feng shui have become widespread in the East.

Not many people realise that feng shui is actually an unfamiliar term to most Chinese people. Learning feng shui is like learning a new language, and it is a language few of the Chinese know. It's easy to see why: the subject was strictly reserved to the powerful and kept secret for thousands of years. And then, later, the practice and use of feng shui was forbidden in China during the Cultural Revolution. Today there are no more than a few surviving classical practitioners who are true masters of the discipline and they wring their hands in despair at the distortion and commercialisation that has occurred in both the East and the West.

We all know what happens when something is marketable. Our need for security, happiness and well-being is big business. Put that together with a human tendency not to learn from our mistakes and you have a guaranteed money-spinner. We want quick solutions and we are becoming less and less critical. Twenty-five or 30 years ago feng shui was completely unknown in the West, but some people managed to create a good business by sticking the label 'feng shui' on everything that had to do with happiness and good luck, cleansing and renewal. Incense, essential oils, music, symbols, amulettes, even toilet paper were marketed as feng shui products.

I often compare the discipline of feng shui to surgery. You probably have a domestic pharmacy at home with creams, plasters, headache tablets, tinctures and herbal poultices, but you know that special expertise is required when a serious accident occurs or you suffer organ failure. That is also true of feng shui: you can tidy and clean up and make yourself comfortable with colours and symbolism and Chinese dragons and coins, but what you do not have is the insight that enables a properly trained feng shui expert to reveal how your house is affecting your life in terms of health and many other things.

Ba gua

As I mentioned earlier, this powerful knowledge was kept secret and often coded so that its methods and insights should not reach the ears of the unauthorised or foreigners or, above all, enemies. When things are written back to front and upside down and then not brought out for many centuries, they are very likely to be muddled. And in our time a great deal of the ancient knowledge has been read and 'understood' upside down and back to front. Things that are hard to understand have been simplified and presented as truths about feng shui. When the teachings about energies, for instance, are seen 'upside down and back to front', it is hardly strange that rational Western minds consider them complicated and ridiculous.

One of the first things that fascinated me about feng shui was what is called the ba gua, the plan with the nine squares. Ba gua means eight trigrams and according to classical feng shui the eight trigrams are located in the eight heavenly directions, as we saw above.

A simplified version exists and you will find it referred to in interior design magazines and popular literature about feng shui. The simplified version, which has spread across the world, disregards both trigrams and directions, the reason being that the significance of the trigrams has not been understood, nor have all the nuances in the close connection between the five elements and the directions. (The ancient texts were at pains to ensure misunderstanding here!) In this simplified, Western ba gua, used in many feng shui approaches these days, eight universal areas of life have been substituted and these are positioned in eight zones of the house.

The only thing you need to do in order to locate these standard areas of life in your own house or apartment is to lay the simple ba gua on top of a plan or sketch of the house and, starting from the wall in which the exit door is located, you will immediately be able to find the zone for money, for romance and love, for honour and prestige and so on. You can then add stimulus to these things with the help of symbols, colours and objects. You don't need a compass; you don't even need to know anything about the direction the house is facing. Many people have tried this simplified feng shui formula and many people have experienced that something really does happen. After all, if you invest effort, enthusiasm, heart and intention to create change and achieve a goal, it is quite obvious that you will be able to make something happen. But that brings us back to short cuts and quick solutions: using this simplified magic, how profound and long-lasting are the changes likely to be?

That was what I was asking myself after trying out the system for a while. Well, it had inspired me to try things on the domestic plane, particularly in the 'money corner' where I tidied things away and placed a tank of goldfish after taking a popular feng shui course during the 1990s. No money turned up, quite the opposite, and the goldfish kept dying on us in spite of looking after them according to all the rules. And as time went on the family was struck by serious illness and unhappiness. Later, when I studied feng shui as a serious discipline, I understand only too well the significance of that aquarium in our lives, being placed just where we had placed it, in the 'money corner'. The point is that during those years a particularly unlucky (and invisible) element influence had settled on or flowed into that part of the house: it was unfavourable earth energy that can contribute to or reinforce illness, bad luck and conflict.

All buildings have different varieties of good and bad influences. For example, there is more than one area in which money or prosperity energy can be activated or stimulated and there are also demanding combinations of elements that can contribute to fires or break-ins. The art is to reveal them and know what can be done to make use of the good and to avoid the bad. Facile and 'magic' solutions end up producing the opposite to what was desired.

An aquarium, for instance, will activate every latent energy and element combination because water in movement has an initiating and reinforcing effect no matter what. And in that case it is of very little help that someone has defined the particular area as a 'money corner'. Simplifications of that kind can be positively dangerous, particularly when water and mirrors are used. So yes, feng shui works...

For thousands of years the characteristics pertaining to direction and time have been decisive and determining knowledge in feng shui. The simplified use of the ba gua does not take any of this into account and it is this form of popularised feng shui that has caused the focus to be so firmly fixed on symbols of good fortune and the purely interior design aspects of the house. The five elements are dragged in at the same time, and colours and forms along with them. The five elements belong to an analysis of the temporal influences of a house, the powerful but invisible influences that can only be revealed by analysing direction and time. In order to do this, you need an advanced feng shui compass and the knowledge how to use it. The position of the house, the use of colours and forms in the various rooms, together with the characteristics of the time period in which we find ourselves – knowledge of all of these is necessary in order to use the five elements as 'medicinal' remedies in a house. Without this insight you run the risk of creating greater problems rather than reducing or getting rid of those you have.

TYPES OF FENG SHUI

It might be helpful to run through the different approaches to feng shui. The over-simplifed approach I've already referred to was introduced in the USA by Lin Yun Rinpoche under the name Black Hat Feng Shui and it quickly became the most widespread form of feng shui in the West. It is presented as being advantageous for people in our part of the world precisely because it has been simplified! Well...

The most important aid is the standardised ba gua described earlier. It is popular in the East, too, presumably because it is very easy to arouse people's interest, easy to link it with symbols and value-laden objects, and consequently easy to earn money using it. No serious master of classical feng shui has ever worked with simplified approaches of that kind.

Another approach is called Eight House Feng Shui which, in short, states there are eight forms of houses and they are characterised by energies that either suit you or don't suit you. The calculations produced by this method conclude that there are two main categories of house – east house and west house – and two main categories of people – east people and west people. Once again the old texts have led to confusion and resulted in a simplified and rather meaningless approach. Classical feng shui treats houses and people as individuals, not as black/white or east/west. All houses and all people are influenced by directions, seasons, climate, fundamental energies and the temporal influences of the elements.

Intuitive Feng Shui is a term that arose in the wake of New Age. It is based on the ability to feel the extent to which a house is good or not. Since we are human beings and since human beings have good days and bad days, no one who recognises the great and comprehensive nature of the discipline of feng shui would recommend that you follow your intuition. After many years' experience practising feng shui it is certainly true that your intuition is sharpened, but a capable practitioner of feng shui will stick carefully to the textbook, just as a surgeon will in the operating theatre.

Even in Scandinavia, simplified systems that claim to have something to do with feng shui have emerged. The very fact of simplification – 'out with the foreign and oriental!' – is used as a selling point in the market place! This really is throwing the baby out with the bath water.

The worst thing of all is the brazen way interior design chains market themselves as experts in feng shui. They offer advice about colours and positioning when all they are doing in reality is selling the latest fashion. People are seduced into believing they are doing something good and important for their lives and health whereas, the results can in fact be fatal.

Form and compass

What gives meaning, has always given and will always give meaning to the true discipline of feng shui are the land forms, heaven directions, climatic conditions and nature that surround us. The use of the compass is regarded as the most advanced form of feng shui, but even with the most advanced calculations and formulae, you cannot get very far if you don't have sufficient knowledge of the influences of forms and landscape.

What is decisive for a good practitioner of feng shui is the ability to perceive how the subtle life energy is moving in the area around a house. How is the house being nourished? Can it breathe? Is it being afflicted by negative influences? Which members of the family are being affected? Is the chi being brought to business premises in a way that will safeguard the business? Does the building have a form capable of stimulating the actual business? How does the energy within the building/house/apartment flow from room to room? Is it retained sufficiently and can it move and circulate freely? All the calculations are made taking account of the kind of influence the chi – the life energy – has on the inhabitants.

Form deals with the landform support around a home or business premises, but also with the form of the house or property – the plan, spaces, room usage, positioning of the house in the terrain, view, neighbouring houses, roads, gradients, trees, lamp-posts, proximity to traffic, airports, rubbish dumps, churchyards, hospitals, industry and so on. Form also deals with the best positioning of beds, desks and stoves. Apart from that, the positioning of furniture as such is secondary in feng shui. What is important to take into consideration is where you spend a long time at any one time. The reason is the invisible effect of the elements and these can be revealed with the help of the calculations of the feng shui compass.

The best feng shui investigations are those carried out by a consultant or adviser who is skilled in both form and compass. Studying form and landscape involves the more visible and noticeable influences, whereas the use of the compass reveals the invisible energy effects that concern the five elements and the connection between time and space. And the fact is that where there is trouble in terms of form, the chi will also be unwilling; and where everything to do with the form is perfect, the chi measurements will be fantastic. The opposite is also true: where the energy is not good enough, the form will be affected by it. Energy follows the form and form follows energy.

It's not particularly unusual to be confused. Authors of feng shui books often make the mistake of wanting to sell their own particular approach, their own views, remedies and solutions at the same time as attempting to explain *everything* they know about feng shui to the reader. You do not learn feng shui from a book, however well written it may be. You can learn *about* feng shui, about what it is and what it isn't, but you learn feng shui by studying the discipline, preferably directly with a feng shui master from Asia, or with someone who has been through such teaching direct from the source.

If you want to study authentic feng shui seriously, you should choose a school that can point to a classical feng shui tradition. It is just the same as when you are referred to a specialist or taken into hospital: you do not go off to the nearest bookshop instead and buy a popular introduction on to how to perform heart surgery on yourself. No, you put your life in the hands of a competent and thoroughly trained practitioner. You should think about feng shui in the same way. Seek out the very best, because it is your life that is at issue!

REMEDIES AND SYMBOLISM

According to fashionable thinking about feng shui, there are numerous feng shui remedies and a host of 'magic' things you can fill your house with to improve life. The truth is that your house does not need to resemble a knick-knack china shop to have good feng shui. (These shops don't have very good feng shui anyway.) On the whole, classical feng shui does not depend on the use of such 'things'. The fact that you have made use of feng shui expertise does not mean it has to be visible – in fact, the only place it should show is in your life!

There are times, however, when a house does need support in energy terms, in which case classical feng shui may recommend using a 'thing' as a solution, that thing being a Buddha support. If a Buddha is out of the question in your garden or house, there are alternatives which are just as powerful. When a house with too little support at its back is helped in this way, everyone who lives in that house is also supported. Support at the back, of course, is particularly important for health and well-being.

Water is also a kind of 'thing'. Water has great power for both good and bad and you need to be aware of what you are doing when you position water in your house or on your property. Sometimes the energy reaching the house and coming in through the door may be so weak that you have to do something to improve the capacity of the house to give life to those who live there. It is sometimes possible to change the situation by making minor adjustments to the angle of the door or the doorframe in order to allow good luck and well-being to enter. Or it may even be necessary to move the door. Sometimes a water installation – an indoor or outdoor fountain – might be the best solution.

Crystals, frogs, wind chimes, spirals, eternity symbols, pagodas, crystal balls, pixies, trolls and flutes are all symbols that mean different things and have different values for individuals, and they are often extremely culture specific. Even though Chinese folklore is full of symbolism, symbolic objects of this sort are not used in serious professional feng shui, not even in China. When terms such as 'tortoise support', 'dragon side' and 'tiger side' occur, they are being used as metaphors for the form phenomena we want to have as supportive elements around a house. Having statuettes of tortoises or pictures of tigers and dragons in the house does not offer any support in life. You are, of course, welcome to have that kind of decor or lucky coins and other symbols to bring joy and hope, but you need to understand that these things have nothing to do with serious feng shui.

Strong and varied colours are also associated with feng shui, and that too is part and parcel of the misconception that feng shui is all about interior decor. Colours can indeed be vibrant and life-enhancing, but a sea of colours at any price is not the same thing as good feng shui. Rather the reverse – strong colours are often too much of a good thing. For instance, if you use red or other colours that belong to the fire element in a room in which the fire element is already too influential, it can have serious consequences. One day there will be a spark – a day, for instance, when the energy of the year and the month add even more fire on top of the invisible fire influences. Suddenly, there is a fire in the house and no one understands why. Or, suddenly, someone has a heart attack and no one has noticed any warning signs.

The colour choices in feng shui must always be made on the basis of the element influences in a room, not on the basis of fashions and trends. Colour choices can reinforce both good and critical influences and – unfortunately – knowledge of this is not to be found in any traditional or modern colour theories but in an understanding of the five elements.

Metal as medicine

The theory of the five elements will be explained later in this book (see Chapter 4). As a feng shui consultant for almost ten years, I have given the following advice to very many clients: use chalk-white! If you paint the walls chalk-white in one or more rooms of the house, you will be using the element of metal as a medicine. It only works where a remedy is really needed: in other rooms the effect might be to make you feel stressed and uneasy – if, for instance, there is already a lot of invisible metal present.

In other words, it's all about using the compass properly and knowing the heaven directions. The metal remedy has been necessary in many houses during the last 20 years because we have been faced with constellations of elements that have caused a great deal of 'sick earth'. If you sleep or sit or work in a room subject to earth influence of that sort, you will become ill, particularly when time energy is knocking on the door of the same room with the same addition of energy. According to the brilliant Chinese theory of the five elements, an addition of metal will have a draining effect on earth. Where we discover too much (invisible) earth, particularly a combination that is hot and unfavourable, the remedy is to paint the walls chalk-white. Metal effects (wallpaper patterns) are also effective, especially when put together with a different element that weakens the earth element – the water element, for instance (turquoise, marine blue, black).

Thus, in years in which the colour fashions have been red or grey, brown, orange or pink, many people have involuntarily ended up choosing a remedy for their walls that is precisely the colour that creates even more burning, sick earth.

When the very centre of the house – 'tai chi', which has a direct effect on the health of those who live there – is struck by this earth influence, it will have unavoidable results in health terms. If the room or rooms in this part of the house are painted in one of the colours that belong to the element of fire, the unfavourable earth influence will reinforce it.

Because of the climate and the position of the sun, very many of the houses in Norway face south-west. The south-west/north-east axis has had precisely this challenging earth influence during the last feng shui period (1996–2016). At times every second consultation I have had has been about 'sick earth' – and illness! The strange thing is that the people in the house have often taken care to keep this earth extra warm and unfavourable, as if illness and misery have become a pattern they may perhaps have been clinging on to. The connections between the house and its residents are subtle and very strong. If illness is knocking on your door and you for some reason don't stand up against it, the house has its ways to agree with you and vice versa. You moved into that particular house with the influences that matched your situation (current or upcoming), and you enhance these influences by adding the colours needed to fulfil your destiny.

The effect is immediately apparent once the remedy is introduced, whether it be by removing a mirror that is reflecting and multiplying the unfavourable influence, or by scraping off red wallpaper and replacing it with white or with metal effects, by removing fire-coloured curtains or carpets, by moving pictures that contain a great deal of red or triangular shapes (fire) to a different part of the house. Those who live there perceive the physical or the mental effect as one of liberation.

Martine and Morten's experience

My partner and I bought a house in the summer of 2014 and set about refurbishing it before moving in. It wasn't until the end of September 2014 that we slept in the house for the first time. By that stage all the walls had been painted, the worn floors had been replaced and things were gradually getting into order. During the first period we were in the house there was no bath so things were rather chaotic well into the autumn. While we were doing the place up there were a great many things that had to be done at the same time and many decisions had to be taken quickly. I can remember feeling that it was all going too quickly and that I didn't have time to think about how I really wanted it. The choice of colours was made quickly and we chose 'cotton', 'light aubergine' and 'Capri', colours which are earth and fire colours, as I've now learnt. If I'd known then what I know now, I would have got in touch with a feng shui consultant before we started anything. Even though we had made many changes to the house, I still didn't feel at home and I felt that something just wasn't right.

After having had feng shui done on the house in the summer we were recommended to do a number of things.

Right at the heart of the house there was a mirror that stood there all day and all night reflecting an untidy open clothes cupboard with coats, caps and umbrellas. Entering the house and going on along the corridor felt difficult. Doors and walls were painted in earth colours. Once we had removed the mirror the whole atmosphere of the room changed. It felt calmer and more pleasant, and after we had also repainted walls and doors chalk-white the room was completely different. It did something for the whole house and the effect was immediate. We had a physical sense that just 'being' was better than before, a nice feeling that is difficult to describe but which you recognise when you feel it. I assume it is because the flow is better and the energy no longer so heavy.

What is even nicer is that other people also comment that it feels so much more open and less oppressive even though they are unable to put their finger on exactly what has changed and without them knowing that we were recommended to 'remedy' the heart of the house. We have changed things, moved the furniture around, tidied up and decluttered. At last I am beginning to feel more at home in the house and sense that things are falling into place.

Sharpened awareness

Learning feng shui or following a consultant's advice in every particular will do something for your senses and awareness. You will begin to notice disharmony in all kinds of ways, whether it be poor maintenance, withered plants, heavy colours, 'poison arrows' or lack of support.

Here is the case of another client:

Everything in the house was earth: walls, furniture, curtains and so on. In addition to that, Reni's measurements showed that the house was affected by heavy, invisible, earth energy. She recommended that we should find remedies for the house. We chose to paint walls and ceilings chalk-white (the recommended 'metal cure'). We had no desire to move the same furniture back in so we bought new. There is no doubt that the energy had been 'lightened' – we noticed the change quite quickly. And the new furniture was nicer.

We have cleared out and thrown away masses of things and that, of course, has also made the atmosphere much lighter. Our place is quite different now and all of us feel much better. It is much easier to keep clean, no bother at all. We have also become much more conscious of the things we want to have around us: simple, smooth surfaces and not so many bits and pieces. Reni also remarked on the kind of symbolism we were surrounding ourselves with in terms of pictures, ornaments and so on – she recommended us to have more variety. This has made me realise how important it is to be 'awake' to the things we have around us. And now that I have a clear, clean colour on the walls around me, I think I see things more clearly and have become more decisive about what I want and where.

New challenges

We are approaching a great, new and different feng shui period (see Chapter 1) which will bring new challenges. We have already experienced a powerful effect, in that time has speeded up or feels as if it has speeded up. Strong heaven energies are on the threshold and we will see elemental conflicts in all buildings.

It is several centuries since this kind of influence surrounded us. Since I have no memory of life lived at that time, I cannot say how it is going to turn out for us. I have to rely on the wise sages who have passed information down through many generations.

A great deal of conflict will be in the air in the coming decades, and knowledge of the flying stars will be very advantageous.

The 'earth period' with stomach trouble, quarrelling, domestic problems, obesity and unhappiness will soon be over, but that does not mean that we stop quarrelling or putting on weight or getting digestive problems or divorcing. Challenges and difficulties are part of being human, but we can actually achieve a good deal by taking hold of our 'man luck' (see Chapter 1) and developing a greater consciousness with regard to choice, values and what and whom we have around us.

The symbolism around us

By using the symbolism with which we surround ourselves, we can consciously reinforce the objects, phenomena and qualities we desire more of in life. We can immerse ourselves in pictures with happy themes, pictures of nature, portraits of people who bring us joy, romantic symbols, erotic pictures, images that symbolise well-being and contentment. Symbols and what they stand for affect us both consciously and unconsciously.

These influences can, of course, be bad as well as good. Many people surround themselves with things they don't even like. Pictures or objects may be displayed out of a sense of duty – they may be gifts or inherited objects, collections of various kinds, conglomerations of porcelain, books, medallions and so on.

It is a good feng shui principle only to have things around you that make you happy. If you are irritated by some knickknack you have on display out of a sense of politeness, that object will be a thief of energy in your life. You can do without that, since we should be able to set our own limits in our own homes and choose freely what we have on display. How valuable and meaningful can a heavy, dark painting be if the only thing it does is to make us depressed?

Not many of us actually realise that it's quite possible to read the life of an individual or family from the symbolism they have around them in their homes. Since we do not take a conscious approach to it, we have a tendency to clutter our lives with collections of the same kind of symbols. A feng shui expert immediately becomes aware of this.

This kind of awareness of symbols is important and can give you a better life. Hang up coins if you like, or display money frogs to your heart's content, but you might just as well start believing in Father Christmas again.

4 HOW TO CREATE FLOW?

When the paths curve as they lead up to the house, the lives of the inhabitants will reveal fewer challenges, more contentment, better health, more success, more luck and more opportunities in life.

THE BASIC PRINCIPLES

In this chapter you will find a hundred or more tips as to what you can do yourself to create a better flow in your home, in its surroundings and consequently in your life. It is always a good idea to take a thorough look outside the house to discover whether it is being influenced in some way. Having the layout and spatial arrangement organised to the highest level does not help much if the house is being seriously affected in some other way.

What follows is an overview of the structural and energetic conditions you should take note of in and around your home, and there are also suggestions for how you can suppress unfavourable influences and reinforce those that are favourable. What we shall focus on here are the energy influences related to form. Invisible influences can only be revealed with the help of compass measurements and calculations. 'Energy follows form' is what we say in classical feng shui and a trained eye is often necessary to understand what is actually going on in energy terms as a result of the effects of form.

Roads and chi

Roads are like rivers, the difference being that the water is replaced by vehicles moving at great speed. There is always a flow in one direction or the other, often in several directions at the same time. A building can receive a good flow of energy from a river or a road, or it can be affected by an influence that is far too strong and consequently negative.

In feng shui terms, roads that curve in a natural and elegant way have the best potential as sources of good feng shui. Straight stretches of road on the other hand will quickly change life energy into a negative, critical influence. We want the activity of a road or of water to be at the front of the house. As mentioned in the first chapter, calm support at the rear of the house offers the best feng shui, whereas active water or a busy road at the back does not provide calm or good support.

STRAIGHT OR CURVING

We want the entrance section to receive fresh new chi from outside in a good and careful way. A straight road running directly towards the entrance door creates a flow of energy that is far too fast. It results in a situation in which the house is virtually overwhelmed and smothered: it is the same kind of effect we experience when we are out in stormy weather and have to turn our faces aside to avoid the sensation of being smothered by the strong wind. The solution here is to slow the direct 'poison arrow' by introducing curves into the pathway or by placing large pots or similar objects capable of slowing the powerful flow of energy.

CROSSROADS AND T-JUNCTIONS

There is no doubt that houses that lie at crossroads receive energy, but they do so in a form that is too powerful and negative. (This is a splendid location for shops and restaurants, however.) The energy reaches the house but it does so too quickly and too forcefully. This is also the case with T-junctions: bright lights from vehicle headlights hit the house all the time and there is a lot of noise. If the driver loses control of his steering, the house is nothing short of a target. In a position like this you are exposed to a rapid flow of energy constantly hitting the house. The solution is to use fences or strong hedges as a barrier.

THE ENERGY FLOWS PAST

When a house is situated on a very busy road, the energy is likely to travel straight past without providing the house with any nourishment at all. This will be even more of a problem if the road is also running downhill past the house. The solution is to try to capture the energy by means of some kind of projecting structure – an arm that can catch and hold on to some of the life energy so that the house can benefit from it.

Y-JUNCTIONS

The energy travels past on both sides without nourishing the house at the same time as the flow of energy directed straight at the house is too strong. Nor is this a good energy situation from the point of view of form symbolism: the house is situated at the cutting point between the blades of a pair of scissors, which can quickly lead to life becoming full of challenges and conflicts.

The solution here is to erect a solid barrier – a fence, hedge or, best of all, a high wall – at the same time as rounding off the property as far as it is possible to do so. If the entrance door is facing the junction, it is worth considering moving it round to one of the sides.

ROADS AWAY FROM THE HOUSE

When there is a road running along one or both sides of the house and it then curves away from the house, well-being, luck and happiness will also disappear. Or the children will leave home and will perhaps stay away for a considerable time.

OTHER CRITICAL CONDITIONS RELATED TO ROADS

If you or your family members are faced with major challenges in life, one important reason could be the influence of 'water' – that is, roads – in the vicinity. Below are some further conditions which it will be useful to be aware of. Both the above and the following points should be borne in mind when acquiring a new home if you want to ensure good feng shui.

Avoid houses situated:

- at the innermost end of a dead-end or at the end of a road
- at a roundabout
- near streets with very heavy traffic
- at street level at a multi-level intersection
- immediately beyond a curve in the road or where the road makes a sharp bend
- in line with a sharp corner, with the point aiming at the house
- with roads surrounding the house on all sides
- in a place where a road circles the house like a noose, or where that kind of noose is immediately opposite.

A more favourable road map

The lives of the inhabitants of a house will have fewer challenges, more happiness, better health, more success, better luck and more opportunities if the roads curve towards the house. If you are thinking of moving, it is a good idea to study a road map of the area first, taking particular note of the following:

- Houses that lie inside a curve will enjoy good energy from the road (or river) without any danger of being affected by negative flows.
- Houses and people are best nourished when the roads in the vicinity have curves and bends. This creates a harmonious flow of energy and is considered to be positive and lucky for the inhabitants and, generally speaking, more favourable than areas in which the houses are arranged as a grid of straight streets.
- A view out over roads and rivers where the water flows calmly has a positive influence.
- A supportive landscape (see Chapter 1), combined with a beneficial energy influence from road or water, determines whether the yin and yang is well balanced in the surroundings. So always check that the house has sufficient support at the back and on each side, either from the terrain or from other buildings. Also, that it is open to the front, but not so open that energy disappears.
- Avoid living on an elevated site without support on any of the sides.
- Avoid living on steep slopes.
- Avoid living in a house where there is a road coming steeply down towards the house.
- Avoid a house situated at the bottom of a depression.

- If you have to climb up many flights of steps to the entrance door, neither you nor the house will be well nourished.
- When there is a set of steps down to the entrance door, energy will reach the door too quickly and forcefully. (Think of energy as water – in this case it would cascade down to the door and into the house.)
- Avoid living right by an airfield, rubbish dump, churchyard or hospital.
- Remove any large rocks from in front of the house, especially those close to the entrance.
- Do not position a swimming pool to the south, south-west, west or north-west of the house.
- Avoid having water behind the house.
- If the house has been extended several times, there is likely to be a confusion of corners and shapes. This can make good feng shui difficult to achieve.
- The same is true of houses in which the different storeys are irregular – for instance, where there are mezzanines and steps everywhere.
- A house with missing corners lacks essential sections from an energy point of view. (Corners are parts of the complete square that contains all the directions, all the seasons and all the trigrams.)
- In a house with more than one entrance door there is a risk that there will be a tendency to speak with more than one tongue. (Gossip and slander, for instance.)

All the things

'If you own more than seven things, the things own you.' So runs an oriental proverb, reminding us that with each thing we bring into our homes we are creating a new tie. We surround ourselves with things, things, things, and we wonder why we do not make any progress in life, why we put off so many things, why we put on weight, why we find it impossible to change. We have mess and disorder all around and yet we wonder why we have so little time, why we squabble, why we are stressed, why we become ill.

Much good feng shui starts with us establishing a conscious relationship with all the things with which we surround ourselves. Are the objects giving you joy and inspiration or are they causing irritation and annoyance? Are you hanging on to gifts and objects for sentimental reasons? Do you have things on display from a sense of duty or politeness? Do you have loads of table settings for reasons that are beyond you? Do you have hundreds of souvenirs collecting dust? Do you have a cupboard full of clothes that might fit you again one day? Are your freezer and your larder full just in case times get hard? What does your shed or your closet, your cellar or your attic look like? Do you spend your time looking for your keys, your spectacles, your driving licence or your wallet? When chaos takes over and you can't keep an eye on everything, things become thieves of time.

You will discover that many things in life become easier if you go through your collections and acquisitions, sort them, weed things out and throw them away. You will almost certainly give yourself more room to breathe and the air will be cleaner. Our houses are extensions of ourselves, they reflect us and we reflect them. In other words, our houses are like living organisms, so try to let them breathe good fresh air, create the best conditions for good, healthy digestive systems and get rid of excesses.

Bring daylight in and ensure there is a good balance between yin and yang. We need both of them and your house will reflect exactly what it is told to: if you draw the curtains and spend most of your time indoors in an apartment decorated in dark colours and with a lack of life and light, it will affect you and make you and your life dark and silent.

Or, for instance, the opposite may be the case: there is too much noise and it's too loud, the colours are too strong and the light through the big windows too bright and merciless. It's difficult to rest in a place like that. If we are to be able to recharge ourselves for a new day in a society that makes high demands on us and is full of stress, we need our surroundings to be more characterised by yin.

FENG SHUI TIPS FOR A BETTER LIFE

Work through your home, area by area and room by room. I guarantee you will notice the differences in your life if you accept the following pieces of advice – they offer important principles for happiness, flow and efficiency at work.

The entrance area
How easy is it to find your house or apartment and the door into it? Energy will reach your home in a good way if the route is easy to follow, so make sure that all visitors are led to your home in an easy and natural way. If you've marked out a clear path to the door, life energy won't have any problems finding its way. So make sure you have:

- clear and obvious signposting
- a house number
- a nameplate on the postbox and entrance door
- a doorbell that works
- a bright and roomy entrance.

Let the energy the house 'breathes in' be as clean and uncluttered as possible. Is the waste bin right outside? Is the entrance being properly maintained? Roots, rubbish, loose flagstones, bicycles and garden tools left lying around will cause energy to be confused, and that affects the house and those who live in it. So make sure you:

- clear away withered plants, rubbish, clutter and anything that creates a mess
- move the rubbish bin away or, if that is impossible, build a neat shed for it
- repair railings, sills, doorsteps, handles and locks, and tighten hinges and screws
- fill cracks in the wall and holes in the drive and repair fences.

The road or path to the house should not point too directly to the entrance door – it should preferably curve so that energy supply is not too vigorous. Use flowerbeds and pot plants to soften the approach – this is the best way of supplying the house with nourishment.

Pots, beds and paving can also be used to advantage in order to mark out clearly the route to the entrance door in the kind of situation, for instance, where the entrance is around a corner and thus invisible from the gate or the drive.

Is there a steep flight of steps immediately outside the entrance door and/or a steep hill? This can be the explanation for a lack of energy and perhaps also for a sense that there is an absence of possibilities in life or that opportunities fail to come through. Try to find a way to raise the level of the area, or create a new approach to the house.

The entrance door

How good is the supply of life energy to your home? The entrance door is the mouth of the house, so is it big enough?

Does the house get enough air? Or too much? An entrance door that opens in a heavy and sluggish way often reveals resistance and an absence of life's opportunities. Check that:

- the door opens easily and without creaking
- the door is obvious and well illuminated, preferably with a lamp on each side: this creates symmetry and the illusion of a face welcoming you
- the door is hung so that it does not push a visitor (and energy) away.

Are there two doors? This often implies that it's easy to develop the habit of speaking with two tongues, so mark one door clearly as the main door and use it most.

The vestibule

This is where the first meeting with you and your family takes place and, as we all know, first impressions are important. If the vestibule is overfull, dark and cramped, people enter the house with a feeling of unease and possibly gain an impression of a lack of openness and neatness. For an active family with children, this area is bound to be a challenge. Time is tight for the parents of small children, so it is all the more important to get plenty of energy. A house capable of breathing will be a great help. So:

- Avoid chaos, heaps of shoes, schoolbags, clothes, empty bottles, old newspapers, rubbish on the way out, overloaded hallstands and hooks full of clothes on the wall just inside the door.
- Narrow passageways make it difficult to breathe, so do not have too much furniture in the vestibule and corridor.

- Make sure there is good lighting.
- Light colours make it feel more spacious.
- Avoid mirrors since they actually multiply the mess, and do not hang a mirror directly facing the entrance door – it will reflect the energy straight back out and the house will be unable to draw breath. And if a mirror image of yourself is the first thing you meet on entering the house, there is a risk that you will experience a past self catching up with you.
- Avoid having a straight line from the entrance door to a balcony or terrace door, a large window or the back door. Life energy will pass straight through and out. Try to restrain it and lead the energy off to one side and through the house by positioning a large plant or folding screen or new door.
- If you have a straight line from the entrance door to a toilet or bathroom or washroom, keep the door of that room closed. Life energy will disappear out with the water rather than nourish the house
- Do you have an internal staircase that points straight to the exit door? The energy that enters the house will be cut by the steps and is likely to have a negative effect on life in the house. (Negative, sharp, cutting energy.)
- The main door and any intermediate doors should be hung on the same side. There is no problem with intermediate doors having windows in them.

The heart of the house

In the middle of the house there is an area – the heart of the house – which is important for the health of the whole family. It is also called the taijii of the house, or tai chi, the balance point.

You can find this area by dividing all sides of the plan into three, taking as your starting point the complete square or rectangle formed when all four outer corners are joined up:

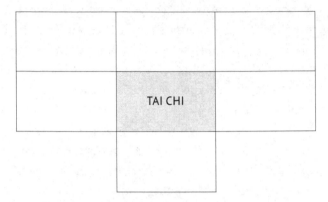

The 'tai chi' is the central square and the actual heart of the house is in the middle of the tai chi. As this illustration shows, the missing corners are always included when the ba gua is drawn. The tai chi should be kept open and spacious if possible. Sometimes there is a bathroom and toilet in this area. Having a room with water in the tai chi is not regarded as lucky because the life energy runs away with the bathwater. Water runs down and in the case of a bath and toilet water is constantly running away. The health of the family will be affected by this – it will, in fact, be drained. The exception to this occurs if there are really unfavourable influences – invisible elements – in the tai chi, in which case these will also be flushed away.

Depending on the layout, the middle of the house can contain rooms of all types – for instance, a corridor with many walls and doors, a bathroom, a staircase. It can also contain several rooms. Irrespective of the layout and construction, however, it is important to ensure that the area is tidy, clean and orderly. So: Watch out for overfull drawers in the chest of drawers. Stacks of post, advertising brochures and newspapers. Drooping plants.

Think about the parallels with your body and health and make sure everything is as it should be. Clogged arteries, blockages, overweight, constipation? Think about preventative measures and keep the area light, clean and pleasant. Put up uplifting and inspiring pictures and symbols in the tai chi. And fresh flowers.

- Avoid placing anything heavy (antique furniture, chests and so on) in the tai chi. Such heavy items can mean that it is hard for the heart to beat and can lead to health issues and challenges for the people who live in the house.
- Is there a fireplace in the tai chi? Ash is clean and fire symbolism is positive for marital and family life. What is bad, however, is to have piles of old newspapers with bad news and negativity. These often end up by the fireplace, which is neither uplifting nor healthy.

Living rooms

This is the place for relaxation, rest, unity, recharging and freedom for everyone in the family. Let there be space for all this – and take a critical look at what it means if the TV rules the roost and determines the furnishings, atmosphere and the opportunities to talk and communicate.

Is there a good balance of yin and yang in the room? (Too light, too dark? See the section on yin and yang in Chapter 4.) Does the furniture allow you to sit securely with good support at your back? Do you have a good view of the room and the door from where you sit?

- Vary forms and colours – the earth element (squares, earth colours) are over-represented in most homes. Round and oval shapes are good remedies against all 'earth' (see the section on the five elements in Chapter 4).

- Avoid too much furniture. Energy should be able to move freely.
- Move the furniture around from time to time to prevent energy stagnating in nooks and corners.
- Use light, neutral colours. Strong colour effects should be restricted to items of furniture, curtains, lamps, etc. It is quite sufficient if one wall has wallpaper with a big, bold pattern. Be sceptical about interior decor trends. Even fashionable colours vibrate and, in the worst case, can lead to major challenges.
- Clean windows provide a clearer view of most things in life.
- Remember to air the house: fresh air and good ventilation renew the energy in the house.
- Fresh flowers contribute fresh, new energy and help us to stay healthy.
- Dispose of withered flowers and dead pieces of plant.
- Do not use dried flowers as decorations – the symbolism refers to death. If you like that kind of decoration, use silk flowers instead. But living plants are best!
- Be careful about using mirrors as wall decorations. Take a critical look at what is being reflected in the mirror – is it really something you want to be multiplied in your life? Might it be the case that what is being reflected all day, day in and day out (a picture with a gloomy subject, muddle and so on), are precisely the things you are trying to get away from in life? Also, all rooms are affected by invisible influences, both good and bad, and there is no reason to multiply the bad if you can avoid it. If you absolutely must have that pretty, favourite mirror on the wall, it would be sensible to get feng shui help.

- Consider the symbolism in the art you have on the walls and shelves of the house. Is there anything that haunts you? Can you see the relationship between the symbols you have around you and the possibilities and challenges facing you?

Kitchens

The kitchen is also a kind of heart for any home since that is where we are fed, preferably with foodstuffs that provide the very best of life energy. Good, healthy food is essential for good health and Eastern traditions stress the importance of family meals being prepared with a calm mind and in a loving and positive spirit. Arguments and conflicts in the kitchen are to be avoided. And for the same reason you should not have a television in that room – it causes anxiety and negativity.

The first rule of feng shui – support – is of particular importance in the kitchen. If the cook is to prepare food that is properly nourishing, he or she must never be exposed to circumstances that might lead to insecurity or loss of energy. This means that the stove should never be positioned in such a way that the cook has to stand with his or her back to the door while focusing on producing wonderful recipes. The most supportive position in any room is one that allows us to survey the whole area. The Stone Age man in all of us is always trying to see what is going on behind him and consequently we are likely to end up wasting a great deal of valuable energy.

The stove itself is of great importance in feng shui – so important that it is advisable to screen it from outside view. The reason for that is to prevent interlopers from intruding, so make sure that the stove is not visible from the entrance door and hall. The stove is the source of welfare, health and growth in the family and it should therefore be protected.

The kitchen is a 'fire room' (see the section on the five elements in Chapter 4) and the stove – logically enough – represents the element of fire. The following points are consequently important and well worth taking note of:

- The stove and the sink – fire and water – should not be too close to each other nor right opposite one another. These positions create disruptions of energy which can lead to conflict.
- Avoid using too much red or other fire element colours in the kitchen. Be careful, too, with water element colours since what we are dealing with is a fire room. (These are navy-blue, turquoise and black.)
- An oval dining table reinforces harmony and the flow of communication.
- Remove the television from the kitchen. It disrupts the preparation of food and the meals.
- Avoid preparing food when you are down, feeling sorry for yourself, angry or in the middle of a quarrel.

Bathrooms

The bathroom is the room for freshening up and cleansing, but it is also the 'waste bin' of the house. According to feng shui, it is unlucky if the layout of the house is such that the door of the bathroom/WC and that of the kitchen are directly facing one another, because it means that incompatible energies are being mixed.

Bathroom, toilet and washroom are 'water rooms'. They have drains and pipes and the water runs down and is sluiced *away*. En suite arrangements with a door directly from the bedroom to the bathroom will have a noticeable effect on the energy level in the bedroom. Dampness from the bathroom can also have a negative effect on the bedroom, so make sure there is good ventilation. Just like human beings, the chi – life energy – can sense the line of least resistance and is more than happy to follow the bathwater out. Consequently:

- If the bathroom, toilet or washroom is close to the entrance door, make sure that their doors are always kept closed.
- If there is a window immediately behind the toilet, the energy will be attracted too rapidly from the door to the actual toilet. Plants hanging down from the window ledge above the toilet can counteract the loss of energy.
- If the bathroom does not have a window, arrange for good ventilation – a fan, for instance – but do not leave the bathroom door open. You do not want fresh energy mixing with what you want to get rid of.
- Should the lid of the toilet be open or closed? In certain circumstances open, in other circumstances closed. This depends on the effect of invisible elements in the room. (A feng shui consultation can provide the answer.)
- Make sure that the WC and the taps are not dripping. Water leaking away often leads to money leaking away.
- Because the bathroom is a water room, too much use of red or other colours from the fire element will lead to a situation where fire and water come into conflict.
- Avoid empty containers on the shelves in the bathroom. Even pretty flasks and pots gather dust and make the flow worse.

Bedrooms

The adult bedroom is one of the most important rooms in the house. The health and well-being of the whole family depend on mother and father – the responsible adults – being in good health and full of energy and initiative. The parents' bedroom should therefore be located in a calm – yin – part of the house, well protected from external influences such as noise and yang everyday activities.

We spend six to eight hours of every 24 in the bedroom so the room has a strong effect on us. Moreover, when we are asleep we are open and vulnerable and thus particularly receptive. In other words, good feng shui in the bedroom is decisive for the quality of our lives.

- Avoid using the bedroom as a work room. The active yang energy will hang in the air and disturb rest and sleep. Remove everything that makes you think of work: laptop, piles of A4 paper, files and folders.
- Bookshelves are disruptive elements in a bedroom. If you are short of space and have nowhere else to keep your books, it's a good idea to keep them behind cupboard doors.
- Having a television in the bedroom is not restful and it continues to be disturbing long after it is turned off. For the same reason, computers, mobile phones and digital alarm clocks should be removed from the bedroom, especially if you are stressed and having problems with sleeping.
- Beds should be positioned with the head end against a completely solid wall, not against a window wall or with the head end out into the room, and absolutely not in the passage between the door and the window. Do have a headboard, and good support at the foot of the bed is also beneficial.
- Have a bedside table on each side of the bed to create balance.

- Avoid having lamps on the wall above your heads. Lamps on the bedside tables are preferable.
- A big heavy picture on the wall above the head end of the bed gives a feeling of insecurity.
- You should not sleep with a structure of shelves above your head. Something could fall down and, purely instinctively, you are likely to be on your guard and waste energy unnecessarily because of the danger overhead. It will have an effect on the quality of your sleep.
- Sleeping with a large lamp or ceiling fan right over the bed is particularly inauspicious. Aggressive paths of energy are created and they affect the body in detrimental ways.
- Avoid piles of clothes and anything else piling up in the bedroom.
- Stop using the space under the bed as a storage space. It leads to stagnant energy which you will then be lying on. If you have to store things under the bed, you should check carefully what it is you are lying on every night.
- The dirty washing basket does not belong in the bedroom, nor do shoes that have been worn outdoors.
- Having a view of the whole room and the door is important.
- Be careful about having mirrors in the bedroom. One plus one does not equal two in the case of mirrors. They reflect the whole time and they create unease and sleeping problems.
- Avoid sleeping under roof beams. Cover them, for instance, with thin and light fabric, or paint them a light colour – the same colour as the ceiling.
- Be aware of sharp edges, projections or corners that point at the bed. Cover them up or rearrange the furniture.

Children's rooms

Children's rooms usually fulfil many different functions – the need for activity, growth, concentration, play, learning and sleep. Children are growing and heading into the world at full speed. They represent an enormous force of yang.

- Use fresh cheerful colours on the walls, but not too strong – strong colours are better used in a painting. Children belong to the wood element (growth), so a child's room painted a strong green can be too much of a good thing and can cause disquiet, particularly if the room is in the east where the wood element is already strongly represented.
- The positioning of the bed is as for bedrooms in general (see above). It is important that a child does not sleep with its head under a window or towards a door and always avoid allowing anyone, big or little, to lie in the area between door and window. The current of energy is too strong there.
- Bunk beds are not recommended. The circulation in both upper and lower bunks is not good and there is pressure from the ceiling on the upper bunk and pressure from the bottom of the upper bunk on the lower bunk.
- Avoid a mess and allowing things to pile up under the child's bed.
- Position the desk so that the child is sitting with its back to the wall. Very few children do their homework at their writing desk, which might be because they instinctively react against sitting staring at a wall. And because they feel uneasy without support at the back.

Work rooms – guest rooms

Combining functions as distinct as guest room and work room is not considered propitious. If you have a home office or work room which you use for extra work or study, a sofa bed ready for an overnight guest will create a conflict of energies which will affect your career ('sleeping career'). The most sensible thing to do then is to decide what the room's main function is. If it is going to be used mainly for work, the best thing to do with the sofa bed is to use it as a spare table, and then, on the rare occasions you have an overnight guest, change everything round.

- Make sure you sit with support for your back and a view of the room and door. The corner diagonally opposite the door is called the 'command position' and that is where you will receive most energy and strength.
- A view out of the window disturbs concentration.
- Looking straight at a wall is uninspiring and bears witness to a blocked future. Your opportunities will become fewer.
- Keep your desk tidy.
- Open shelving leads to disturbed energy. Place any folders and papers you are not using in closed cupboards and drawers so that you do not waste energy by being constantly reminded of all the other things you ought to have done.
- Having a mirror in the work room also disrupts the energy, especially if you can see your reflection from where you are sitting.

Internal staircase

A staircase inside the house is a space shared by all the family. Let the images on the walls be things that encourage and bring joy to adults and to children. Do not place things on the steps – that always creates a poor flow and there is also the risk of tripping.

- Open steps on the staircase? Energy disappears between the steps and never reaches the upper floor. Life energy is needed in all rooms, so – if possible – seal between the steps.
- A spiral staircase? The energy becomes sharp, intense and confused. Instal a good light at the very top and it will help to draw the energy up.
- A window on the staircase can confuse the energy and make it disappear out instead of continuing up or down. Glaze it with coloured or smoky glass.
- If you are going to put in a staircase and are in a position to choose the number of steps, choose an odd number (3, 5, 7, 9, 11, etc.). Odd numbers are yang and even numbers (2, 4, 6, 8, 10, etc.) are yin. When we are on a staircase we are in movement and movement is yang. In this way you can create a better agreement between form and energy – one of many interventions we can make so that existence is character-ised more by harmony than disharmony.

YIN AND YANG – THE ART OF FINDING THE BALANCE

As described earlier, the concept of yin and yang is central to the Chinese culture and tradition in which the discipline of feng shui originated. The yin-yang symbol expresses a state of perfect harmony and balance, of equilibrium and it is an image of light and shade.

Without the sun, we would not have shade, and precisely because there is a strong sun we are very happy that there is something called shade. Without the life-giving sun, life would not exist on our earth, but the sun would kill all life if we had no chance to protect ourselves against it and cool down when necessary. This is true for all forms of life on this planet, not just for mankind.

The symbol has a light side (yang) and a dark side (yin). The two forces lie wrapped around one another almost like two foetuses in the same womb. And this is a very precise image, for each and every one of us, irrespective of whether we are a man or a woman, contains both forces. The dance of yin and yang is going on within us all the time – opposite forces in a state of mutual dependence.

The symbol has another, rather mystical aspect: the two dots – the black in the white and the white in the black. This reveals to us that yang always contains the seed of yin and yin always contains a yang force waiting to emerge.

Copyright © Janabehr, Dreamstime.com

First there is a motionless state of tension, two poles, two opposite forces, and yin and yang grow in this state. Life arises and motion begins and this motion continues constantly within the closed circle: a mutual dance of opposites. Yang withdraws and allows yin to grow; yin diminishes and yang grows. Everything – objects, beings, events – grow and develop in time with the changes between yin and yang.

Night and day

Thus, great things and small things can be explained in the light of yin and yang, the most obvious of all being night and day. We are all familiar with the darkness of night and with its direct opposite, broad daylight. Yin and yang also stand for the sun and moon. But what is yin and what is yang? Is the day yin or yang? Is it the sun that is yin or is it the moon? The symbol has a dark side and a light side – which of them represents yin and which represents yang?

The well-known yin-yang symbol is precisely that, a symbol of balance and harmony. This is what the Chinese characters for yin and yang look like, with yin on the left and yang on the right:

$$陰 陽$$

The Chinese character for yang presents an image of the sunny side of a ridge and represents light, warmth, sun and life. This is what the sun offers. The light part of the yin-yang symbol stands for yang: life, activity, strength, action. The yin character presents the shady side of the ridge and it represents shade, respite, calm and stillness, qualities that are equally desirable. The dark side of the symbol is yin.

The light side of the symbol is yang and the dark side yin. There are many women who are more than a little confused when they hear this. Most people have regarded yin as associated with the feminine side and yang with the masculine side, and yet people tend to think that the feminine side is light and bright whereas the masculine is quite the opposite. If we think of the association between the moon and the feminine, it all becomes clearer and more logical. Yin is the 'moon side' of the symbol – the darkness of night. Yang is the 'sun side' – light, active day.

However, both men and women are bearers of light and dark and consequently are both yin and yang. There is nothing that is exclusively yin or completely yang. And there is nothing that is completely black (dark) and nothing that is completely light, however much it shines. Everything bears within it the seed of the opposite, or of the necessary other side of the truth. Your shadow may not always be visible, but it is there all the same.

Cycles

According to Eastern thinking, everything in existence is affected by cycles. Cycles and cyclical movements – patterns that recur – are, of course, what comes to mind when we look at the circular yin and yang symbol.

There is a black spot in the middle of the light semicircle and an equivalent white spot in the middle of the black semicircle. This is an image of the fact that yin is always ready to be born and grow in yang and the equivalent yang seed is lying ready in yin. Yin always contains yang and yang always contains yin. In the cyclical process from yin to yang and back again, the forces dance, exchange, struggle, fuse and even conflict with one another.

We can see this in absolutely everything around us once we have understood the phenomenon: the dawn of day, the start of the new year, new life – all of this is the rebirth of yang. It is life. Life desires life and growth desires nothing other than growth. There is no better image of yang than a small child growing: it has so much yang force that its level of activity exceeds that of every adult. At the same time, however, the road to yin is never shorter than when the little child is at its most yang, when, in a flash, the child falls into a deep sleep.

The new day bathes in fresh energy from the rising sun and this is the most life-giving force we know – the light wakes us and gets us moving. It causes plants to shoot and provides the precondition for warmth, activity and survival. The same is true of the New Year: even before spring is visible, new life is on the way and ready to wake, germinate, grow and ripen.

We all long for summer, for sun and warmth, and cold, wet days make us irritable. But we know in our hearts that the shady side is absolutely necessary. Without cool, particularly without rain and water, we should have very little chance. After an hour in the roasting sun on the beach in some southern paradise we waste no time in heading for the pool or for the cooling waves. The sun is the most yang force we know: its burning heat is merciless, but it is completely essential for things to germinate and grow. And water? As we all know, water is the most important precondition for life on this planet. So water must surely be yang, too?

Fire and water

The concept of fire and water is a matter of opposing forces: 'fire and water', 'dog and cat', 'woman and man'. As we have seen, fire is yang; water, as such, is actually yin.

It becomes easier to understand if we think of climatic conditions.

Water freezes to ice in the middle of the winter and a snow-covered landscape which is still and virtually motionless is just about as yin as it is possible to imagine. Yang means life and activity; yin means stillness and death (in the cyclical sense that the seed of new life is safely preserved in the phase called 'death'). Yin is dark, mysterious and black (the black part of the symbol); is there anything darker, more mysterious and black than the depths of the ocean? Water is yin and fire is yang.

But there is also the fact that everything is relative, and this means that yin and yang are even more fascinating as concepts. There is a huge difference between a hidden, calm lake with a mirror-like surface and the thundering waterfall over the next ridge. The main ingredient of both is water, but whereas the lake undoubtedly has yin quality, the waterfall is full of life, movement and action – and consequently is yang.

The light of the moon does not make anything grow, and the moon – in spite of its light – is typical yin. The light of the moon is, of course, due to the light of the sun. But does the moon lack power? Most of us have noticed that moon power exists and that it is still, black and yin. But is it weak? Certainly not. The cycles of the moon have great influence on many processes on our planet. When we associate the energy of the moon with women's power and emotions, it is not just a polite, romantic notion; it is an expression that yin is also a power and that the moon is part of the eternal dance of yin and yang.

Sun and warmth are the very symbols of life and activity, but they can also be the cause of the opposite. Burning heat and desert conditions create not life but parched death. When something becomes too yang, yin is not far away.

Such are the cyclical processes. When something is at its most yang, the next stage is already a fact and yin is starting. However warm and bright it may be in the middle of the day, a moment later things are moving towards afternoon, evening and night. And when night is at its darkest, yang is already waiting and the seed of the following day is in the process of being born: it grows lighter, the dawn creeps in and day becomes a fact.

Fire can also be both yang and yin. Most of us have few problems with the small flames of candles. We need this kind of energy in the darkness of autumn and during the cold winter periods when we have very little daylight, sun and warmth. The world is cold and yin in the middle of the winter, particularly up here in the north. The flames of lighted candles create atmosphere, warmth and light, and the contrast is obvious – yin becomes yang. Compared with a great blaze or a forest fire, the small flame of the candle is anything but yang – it is yin. It is small and it can be extinguished by no more than a puff of wind. But at the same time we know it has inherent inner strength and that the small flame is all that is needed to start a great fire. At that point fire has definitely moved from being yin to being yang and such a fire results in anything but life: when the blazing house is extinguished, everything is black.

The study of yin and yang is important and useful in the discipline of feng shui. The right condition between yin and yang is decisive for a good balance of energies. When yin and yang are in balance, it becomes possible to achieve growth and change. This is an important goal in feng shui.

Yin	Yang
moon	sun
night	day
evening	morning
afternoon	forenoon
winter	summer
autumn	spring
water	fire
darkness	light
stillness	loudness
passive	active
low	high
weak	strong
small	big
soft	hard
cold	hot
damp	dry
back	front

down	up
adult	child
old	young
dying	newborn
reaping	sowing
slow	fast
heavy	light
careful	rash
sick	healthy
chronic illness	acute illness
alkaline	acid
even numbers	odd numbers
countryside	city
compression	extension
walk	run
stay	go
burnt out	hyper
receive	give
negative	positive
playfulness	rationality
multiplicity	onesidedness
introverted	extroverted
feminine	masculine

Imbalance

More than ever before the world is in need of knowledge of yin and yang. We see imbalance everywhere. It shows in the economic crisis, disasters, famine, persecution, terror, hate, suffering, tyranny, sorrow and loss. Abundance and poverty, greed and resignation live side by side on our planet.

The world is being driven by an insane yang force and the call is more, more and me, me. We are dragged along in this crazy merry-go-round and more and more of us are feeling that our bodies are stressed and burnt out.

We are living in a time of yang, an age characterised by yang attitudes. The only thing that matters is getting from one point to another as fast as possible. We are faced with a veritable queue of demands and challenges and we have no choice but to run in several directions at the same time. We are supposed to be productive, efficient, constantly active in every area. The demands for efficiency are enormous, the pace is hectic. We must be on top form, know the right people, be capable of the right things, be active and up-to-date, however worn and exhausted we may be. 'Tired and weary? Try our energy drink!' 'Mid-life crisis and starting to feel the problems of ageing? Enter a mountain-bike marathon!' Yet another goal to set yourself, yet another run from Point A to Point Z, to yet another finish line, one more boundary broken – preferably as the outright winner.

When do we ever listen to our bodies, to nature? We have become experts in not listening in spite of the fact that there is noise around us all the time. Or perhaps that is why? Noise at work, on the bus, in the shop, in the lift, at our neighbours, in the street, at the gym, in the park, in the woods. Where can we possibly find stillness?

What we need in an age so marked by yang is not some energy drink that will make us even more hyper and yang. We need to achieve balance for ourselves and our surroundings. We need yin and we need it now before we end up totally shattered and exhausted in a black night. Burn-out is spreading. Is that odd? For a variety of yang reasons, someone who is burnt-out tumbles headlong from a position in which everything is at its most yang down into a black hole – yin. There are some people who then need years in order to achieve balance, to get back on their feet and start living again.

How to achieve better balance

In other words, an awareness and knowledge of yin and yang is enormously important and the responsibility for achieving balance in life is no one's but our own. And it is not necessarily that difficult:

- For example, *prioritise* starting the day in a good way for the whole family, taking the time for a calm and pleasant breakfast in order to move on into the day without stress.
- Allow yourself to daydream in the course of the day – it provides an excellent break for an overheated brain.
- Breathe! Set your telephone or computer to alert you at regular intervals that it is time to take deep, slow breaths.
- Take a shower when you arrive home from work in order to wash away all the stress. Symbolic actions of this kind are more effective than you give them credit for.
- Choose fitness programmes that are more yin than the vigorous type desired by many people. Slow walks during which you take in nature and your surroundings with all your senses are good yin medicine.
- Nature offers strong, preventative yin medicine, and it works for everyone – the prescription is green and free. And you can bring nature into your home: an excellent balance can be achieved by surrounding yourself with natural materials in terms of decor, furniture, bed-covers and so on.
- Green is the most life-giving colour in the world. It is also the colour that creates the greatest natural harmony – and there are endless shades of green.

- Green plants have an amazing ability to ensure a healthy indoor climate. All green plants give off oxygen and there are some species that also cleanse harmful substances from the air. Fast-growing plants with large leaves and which need large quantities of water are the most effective when it comes to purifying the air. Recent studies demonstrate that large green plants in office environments lead to a lower rate of airborne infection among the employees. In high-density modern apartment blocks air quality can be a problem and we are afflicted by many kinds of molecule from solvents, plastics and other chemical substances. Green plants can function as cleaners for us: different plants are effective for different substances, so it is worthwhile having many varieties of plant. But avoid having green plants in the bedroom – they produce carbon dioxide at night and we need to be breathing pure oxygen in the room where we sleep and recharge our batteries.

- Yoga, tai chi, qi gong and other forms of spiritual practice, particularly meditation, are activities that help reduce stress and induce spiritual and physical calm.

- A good cup of tea will give you the yin calm you need when you are trying to get rid of symptoms of stress. Alcohol appears to be de-stressing but in reality it has a yang effect on the physical system. Coffee wakes you up and keeps you going, but cup after cup eventually has the opposite effect, leaving the physical and nervous system stressed and exhausted and completely out of balance.

- If you are down and feeling sorry for yourself, it is a good idea to let in the daylight, open the way for the fresh new energy from the east in the morning. And make sure that the imagery you have around you is not contributing to dragging you down even more.

- Plants with long trailing stalks and leaves are perhaps not the best things to raise your spirits.
- Things that pile up around you contribute to dragging you down and holding you back.
- Disorder and an excess of things are expressions of blocked energy.

Burn-out?

If you are so weary and burnt out that you can't face the thought of undertaking anything at all, or if you know someone in that situation, it is particularly important that you ensure that the bed and the bedroom is a place that slowly but surely can help build you up.

- Make sure you have soft bedclothes, preferably made of natural materials that do not irritate the skin. Our skin is our major sensory organ and for someone who is already over-sensitive and feeling low, it is essential that nothing should make the situation worse.
- Keep the bedroom clear of everything that reminds you of things you ought to have done: memos, shopping lists, bills, unread newspapers and magazines.
- Avoid letting things pile up. Get help to clear the bedroom of everything that is unnecessary and make it a good safe zone.
- It should be light but not too light. And don't forget to air it!
- Above all, someone who is utterly worn down should have the bed positioned so that they are getting effective first aid from feng shui's first rule: Support!

    Without support we are drained of life force. As far as the bedroom is concerned, support means that the bed should be positioned with its head against a whole wall. And having a good headboard is also helpful.

Alertness

Too much and too little are often equally bad. Be suspicious of fashions and trends – it's better to find out what will really be good for you. A knowledge of the influence of nature on everything that lives is a good and clever starting point. Feng shui is everything around us, so be attentive and alert to all the influences around you. It might be helpful here to repeat the most important principles of feng shui:

- The entrance area and the entry door facing an active outdoor area bring in life and activity.
- Don't cause the house to have breathing problems. Make sure that things are tidy, pleasant and well-kept outside the entrance door and in the vestibule.
- A constricted and overfull vestibule with mirrors that reflect the disorder cuts off the breath before it has any chance of nourishing the rest of the house.
- The kitchen, children's room and home office are yang rooms and their natural position is close to the entrance at the front of the house.
- The parents' bedroom should be in a withdrawn position in a yin part of the house.
- The living room has to nourish the whole family and provide both rest and refreshment. Avoid having windows that are too large – they make a room too yang, especially if they face south/south-west.
- Too few windows with too small an area do not allow in enough light and life energy. They create a yin atmosphere which can lead to passivity.

- Avoid the colours blue and black in bedrooms, especially if the room lies in the north (water element – see the section on the five elements below). This can contribute to or reinforce tendencies to depression.
- Strong colour effects are yang and are not recommended on the walls in any room. Use neutral, soft and light colours on the walls and stronger colour effects on curtains, cushions, lampshades and the like. An attractive wallpaper is good and effective, but only on one wall.
- Good lighting is an excellent way to create a balance of yin and yang. Natural daylight is important for all life, including human beings.
- Light from the east – the fresh, new, rising energy that flows over us every morning – is priceless. Try to open a way for it to enter your home.
- Fresh air: good ventilation boosts energy and creates a healthy yang atmosphere.
- There is more get-up-and-go in things if the furniture is moved a few inches out from the walls: this allows the life force to reach motionless, yin corners.
- Find ways around the house to capture the good life energy. This means, above all else, finding supportive forms and structures. Try to prevent energy escaping from your house. Chi – the life energy – moves like water. It can flow and cascade downwards but has serious problems making its way uphill.

FIVE ELEMENTS – A COLOURFUL PLAN

I mentioned in the first chapter that the theory of the five elements lies at the heart of most of what we find inspiring about Eastern wisdom: philosophy, the art of living, acupuncture and other forms of healing. Through an understanding of the fundamental processes – or the movements expressed by the five elements – it is possible to work out the reasons for imbalance and consequently restore balance. That is precisely what feng shui aims to do. Feng shui deals with organising things in such a way as to make our surroundings healthier. The goal is a better life.

The influences we are subjected to, or to which we subject ourselves, are either created by man, or they can be of an earthly kind, or strike us from above. We can see a great deal with the naked eye: steep slopes, beautiful ridges, views of water, power lines, the corner of our neighbour's house pointing at our door; and we can hear and smell too, particularly the shrill voice of our neighbour and the reek of his barbeque, or the noises of the town and sirens, as well as the twitter of birds and the babbling of the brook. But the 'atmospheric' heaven energy is neither so easy to relate to nor to understand, because, of course, we cannot see it. Nevertheless, it has the power to bring about both healing miracles and crushing devastation. According to Chinese wisdom, the five elements in yin and yang form affect and govern absolutely everything and it is possible, given a knowledge of the five elements, to interpret and to master the life force. An expert in feng shui is like an energy doctor examining a patient – the patient being the house. With the help of keen observations and measurements with the advanced feng shui compass, the condition and influence of the life energy and five elements on the place are revealed, and this enables us to make a diagnosis.

The five elements – wood, fire, earth, metal and water – all have a particular relationship with one another and they occur in cyclical processes that may be creative, controlling or draining. They are part of the circle dance of yin and yang, and it is this dynamic that leads to the creation and existence of life in the world – living, enjoying, creating, loving and struggling.

The cycles of the elements

All life depends on fertile earth and Mother Earth is constantly turning on her axis. The earth element is the midpoint of everything. The other four elements – wood, fire, metal and water – are associated with the heaven directions: east (wood), south (fire), west (metal) and north (water). The sub-cardinal directions are also associated with the elements: south-east (wood), south-west (earth), north-west (metal) and north-east (earth; see also Chapter 1). These connections are an important part of the set of tools at the disposal of the feng shui consultant.

In addition to the elements being linked with the heaven directions, they are also connected – as we mentioned earlier – with the seasons of the year and the phases of the day. The cyclical processes that embrace the movements and the interrelationship of the five elements are perhaps best understood in the light of changing seasons and our divisions of the 24-hour period of the day. After winter (water) comes spring (wood), which needs warmth (fire), and so on. This is the nourishing, creative cycle – see below.

The controlling aspect is just as important: fire spreads rapidly in all directions and we need water to douse it. The growth of wood needs to be controlled and we need metal when we cut the grass and prune fruit trees, for instance. The controlling element cycle is given on page 151.

There is also a draining cycle in which the element drains or weakens the foregoing element (see page 152).

The arrows that go clockwise in the circle illustrate the nourishing, creative cycle (harmony):

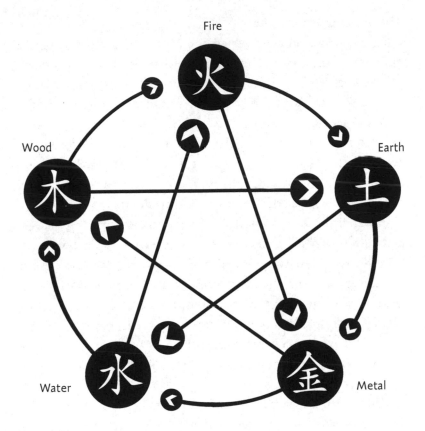

WOOD	Wood burns and feeds fire.
FIRE	Ash from the fire nourishes earth.
EARTH	Processes in earth create minerals and metals.
METAL	The element metal enriches water with minerals.
WATER	Water nourishes plants (wood) and makes them grow.

The arrows in the middle show the controlling cycle (polarity/opposites):

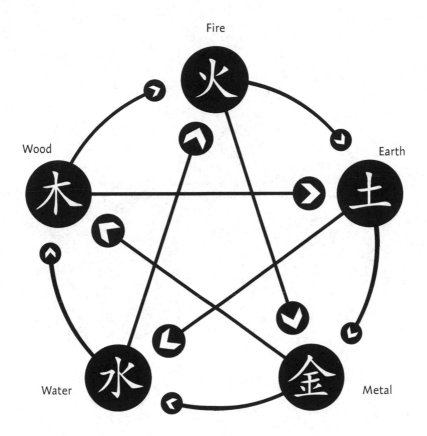

Copyright © Thomas Hagen Kaldhol

WOOD   With their roots, plants can cling on and impoverish earth.

FIRE   Strong fire can melt metal and make it flow.

EARTH   Earth can take up and absorb water, and dams can hold back water.

METAL   Metal in a refined form can chop wood.

WATER   Enough water can extinguish fire.

In the draining cycle the arrows in the circle illustrate a draining or impoverishment of the foregoing element:

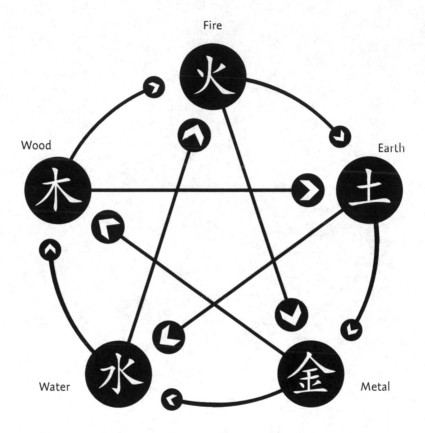

Fire

Wood

Earth

Water

Metal

Copyright © Thomas Hagen Kaldhol

WOOD	Water is sucked up by wood.
FIRE	Wood is burnt up by fire.
EARTH	Ash is absorbed by earth.
METAL	Earth is impoverished when minerals are formed.
WATER	Minerals (metal) are taken up by water.

Yin is mother and yang is father

The five elements are born in the interplay between yin and yang and can best be seen as yin and yang in motion. Yin is mother and yang is father and the five elements are their children. Mother is Mother EARTH and father is Father METAL. Earth energy is what we are all dependent on to exist and survive. Metal energy is associated with heaven energy, and all of us on this planet are at the mercy of it. We look up and we see clouds, sun, moon, stars, rain, snow, birds and insects. We look down and we see puddles, tarmac, sand, mud, grass, weeds, artificial turf, gravel and moss. We human beings and all living things exist halfway between the stars and the puddles.

The following pages provide an overview of the five elements and what they are associated with.

Wood

The element wood represents rising life energy: the fresh, new energy every morning; the force of growth in spring; the growing child keen to learn.

COLOURS:
Green; all shades of green.

FORMS:
Tall slim forms (tree trunks, tower blocks); rectangles standing on end.

OBJECTS:
Plants; trees; tall pieces of furniture (but not panelling, parquet, wooden materials – all these are dead wood, not growing wood, and therefore count as earth element).

SYMBOLISM/CHARACTERISTICS:
Growth; the urge to investigate; innovation; enthusiasm; joy; communication; signals.

TRIGRAMS:
Thunder; first son; yang wood; east.
Wind; first daughter; yin wood; south-east.

FIRE

The fire element stands for the most powerful yang force we know – the heat that all of life is dependent on but also needs to protect itself against. The hot summer months; ripening; the young adult coming into full bloom.

COLOURS:
Red; pink; orange-red; lilac; sky blue.

FORMS:
Points; pointed shapes; pyramids; triangular shapes.

OBJECTS:
Wax candles; hearths and fireplaces; stoves; red effects.

SYMBOLISM/CHARACTERISTICS:
Romance; love; warmth; togetherness in pairs; passion.

TRIGRAM:
Fire; second daughter; south.

EARTH

Earth in itself is the transitional element – it occurs as the bridge between the four seasons and, similarly, the parts of the 24-hour period. Its important function is to contribute to a good transition from one element to another. In human life, the adult responsible for supervision at home and at work.

COLOURS:
Yellow; orange-yellow; brown; beige; grey.

FORMS:
Low forms; squares; rectangles lying on the long side.

OBJECTS:
Ceramics; porcelain; stone figures; the classic sofa; chests of drawers; everything four-sided; tiles.

SYMBOLISM/CHARACTERISTICS:
The nourishing principle; care; mother/child; solidarity; fellowship; games with rules.

TRIGRAMS:
Earth; mother; yin earth; south-west.
Mountain; youngest son; yang earth; north-east.

METAL

The element metal represents diminishing life energy, from the day at its height through afternoon and evening to sunset; the months of autumn; the elderly person who is beginning to direct his/her attention more inwards.

COLOURS:
White; metallic decor and details.

FORMS:
Round; oval.

OBJECTS:
Things made of metal – frames, prize cups; a circular metal wall-clock; coins; metal instruments; handles; metal ornamentation.

SYMBOLISM/CHARACTERISTICS:
Precision; concentration; order; sound; musicality; introspection; sorrow.

TRIGRAMS:
Heaven; father; yang metal; north-west.
Lake; youngest daughter; yin metal; west.

WATER

The water element stands for the winter months and cold, peace, stillness and death; yin. Nature has apparently fallen completely silent. The year is moving to its conclusion, human life likewise. But the seed of yang lies in yin and new life is born of water.

COLOURS:
Navy blue; black; turquoise.

FORMS:
Wave shapes; uneven shapes.

OBJECTS:
Aquarium; fountains; vases; wave-shaped objects.

SYMBOLISM/CHARACTERISTICS:
Births; depth; intelligence; flexibility; movement; water themes.

TRIGRAM:
Water; middle son; north.

In and around us

As always, the aim of feng shui is to create balance. A practitioner of classical feng shui is in a position to uncover the five elements which are present in invisible form in a house. Together with a knowledge of yin and yang and how the life force (chi) occurs, feng shui has powerful methods that enable it to create flow and balance.

Given our cultural background, it is perhaps difficult to understand that the effects and consequences of invisible influences can be momentous and decisive for much of life. But even though we may not see and recognise the connections, they are there all the same. For good or bad, our homes and their surroundings have an effect on us.

Each and every one of us is composed of the five elements in a unique way, with a particular element dominating us and the sort of lives we have. Because feng shui is both time and space, the time at which we were born will be significant for who we are. Every single day has a unique combination of elements, which means that the day on which you were born is decisive for the kind of life you will have.

Knowledge of this is a particular branch of feng shui and a competent consultant will always take the individual's combination of elements into consideration when carrying out a consultation about the house. The personal feng shui analysis, which is based on the eight signs at the moment of birth (see Chapter 2), resembles the feng shui analysis of a house: Which elements are dominant? What is the balance between yin and yang? What can be done to create a better flow, better balance, a better life?

What kind of traits, 'energy' and potential health issues do you have? In the overview above, can you see the connection with one or more elements? What is your type? Do you worry a lot and, at the same time, are you a caring, giving person who likes to function as a peacemaker? In that case you are probably strongly marked by the earth element. Or are you melancholy, with a tendency to introversion? Or full of drive and initiative, with lots of ideas and enthusiasm? The table below will give you some ideas.

Very few people, if any, have a perfect, balanced make-up. We are, after all, human and we all have strong sides and weak sides. Life offers us opportunities and challenges and we have our ups and downs. The theory of the five elements, however, is a powerful aid and can inform us about personality, health, weaknesses, strengths and many other things.

Element	Wood	Fire	Earth	Metal	Water
Organs and body parts	liver, gall bladder, eyes, sinews	heart, arteries, small intestines	stomach, spleen, rectum	lungs, colon	kidneys, bladder, reproductive organs
Feelings	joy, anger	passion, hysteria	care, anxiety	concentration, sorrow	intuition, fear
In balance	positive	lively	generous	analytic	talented
Out of balance	negative	confused	over-protective	over-disciplined	suspicious
Strength	expansion	fusion	moderation	contraction	consolidation
Movement	upwards	all directions	gathering	inwards	flowing
Desire	purpose	fulfilment	fellowship	order	mysticism
Will	resourceful	communicative	willingness to negotiate	discriminating	imaginative

The five elements have innumerable aspects. The above table shows some of the connections between an individual's personal characteristics and the influences of the elements.

A feng shui horoscope, for instance, can reveal whether there are health aspects you need to be particularly attentive to, whether there are particular activities or career directions that might contribute to creating a better balance of elements in your life and thus lead to enhanced well-being. You would be able to gain an insight into whether there are particular challenges ahead and how you can strengthen and protect yourself. Or, perhaps, the opposite: does your fate have opportunities and better fortune in store for you during the coming years and what is the best way for you to seize those opportunities?

There are many people who sneer at astrology and others who want nothing to do with things determined by fate. The Chinese have been familiar with the five elements for thousands of years and, culturally speaking, they have been less concerned about fate as something frightening and dangerous and more interested in fate as luck. A feng shui horoscope can predict such things as whether life will proceed smoothly or whether it will present mountains to be climbed, what career possibilities will be available to you, whether you will have to struggle to earn your daily bread, whether you will be lucky or unlucky. It can tell you whether and when a partner might appear, even whether there are several partners lined up, whether you will have children and, when they come, whether your partner will abandon you.

There is less chance of ending up as a victim of difficult events and circumstances if you understand what is going on and can do something about it, either by averting something undesirable or by moderating the effects of a problem. Chinese astrology, particularly the form of analysis called ba zi ('eight signs') which practitioners of classical feng shui have in their armoury, is the perfect tool to gain insights of this kind. You can then use what you know to make the necessary provisions and to undertake changes that can be life-saving. In practice this will involve you ensuring you have the best possible feng shui and then following the advice offered in the horoscope.

The elements and the house

Even with the elementary knowledge of the five elements given here you will be able to think about the colours and forms in your house in a new way. Look around and notice which form is most dominant in the place you live: like most other people, you will realise that it is the square. This is the typical earth form. There will be no shortage of earth forms in your home, that's for sure. In addition to that, your walls will probably be painted one of the currently popular shades of cream, eggshell white, latte coffee or something similar. Even more earth. So the next time you are redecorating, you can create better balance and harmony around you by varying the forms slightly: introduce a circular mat on the floor, or a picture with an oval motif in it, or a round or oval dining table – the dominant earth element will be modified by these metal forms. The metal energy will wear down or 'drain' the earth energy (see the cycle of the elements on page 151).

According to classical feng shui, the internal walls around us are the key feature when it comes to remedying an imbalance of elements. The walls of a room are like a cloak that we put on and the colours vibrate and affect us. An overly powerful metal influence from the five elements might, for instance, cause anxiety and stress (unless the metal is part of a feng shui remedy against an unfavourable earth influence) and the colour we choose when we paint or paper the walls can either reinforce or weaken this influence.

Since the elements are also linked to the directions, a knowledge of this will provide an excellent and effective possibility for variation and a better energy flow:

Element	Direction	Colour	Form
Wood	east, south-east	green – all shades	towering, tall rectangle
Fire	south	red, pink, lilac, orange-red, sky-blue	triangular, points
Earth	centre, north-east, south-west	yellow, orange-yellow, brown, beige, grey	square, lying rectangle
Metal	west, north-west	white, metal, metal effects and details	round, oval
Water	north	navy-blue, black, turquoise	irregular, wavy

A bedroom (yin – sleeping is rocking in the element of water) in the north (yin, water) done out in blue (water) will produce a water influence that is too strong. It will also be too yin and you risk waking up feeling miserable and that can develop into depression. It would be sensible to moderate the water element somewhat: if you introduce some wood element, it will drain the water; fire will also tone it down, and earth will control it.

The kitchen is a fire room because the stove represents strong fire, and this is the room in which fire is used to nourish the whole family. If the kitchen lies in the south (yang, fire) of the house, it can all become too much, especially if too much colour belonging to the fire element is used. You should, in any case, avoid too much red in a kitchen because water is also an important element in that room. Fire and water are conflicting energies and too strong a presence of such energies – even if they are invisible – can reinforce existing conflict and disharmony and even cause new conflicts.

If you are thinking of redecorating the children's room, bear in mind that children are characterised by the element wood (growth, inquisitiveness, development), so having green walls in that room can be too much of a good thing. If, additionally, the room lies in the east, there will naturally be a great deal of yang wood energy simply as a result of the direction. In that case, any colour but green would be preferable.

In much popular literature about feng shui you will find advice that differs from the above. There is a widespread misunderstanding that a room needs the element that naturally pertains to the direction in which it is situated. The direction is already affected strongly by the element – metal in the west, for instance – and rooms in that part of the house do not need more metal. If you have chalk-white walls in a room in the west, it creates a cold atmosphere and, moreover, in the feng shui period we have behind us, many layers of invisible metal have been present in west rooms. There is actually too much of it and it has been the cause of stress. If you add chalk-white walls or other types of metal on top of this, depending on the type of room in question, you will be encouraging challenges and problems. Even at best a solution of this sort would make it impossible to be at peace.

Another widespread misunderstanding is that the more red there is, the better the feng shui. The colour red is very important in Chinese folklore and superstition and it is reckoned to be a protective colour. That does not necessarily mean that a red entrance door is a guarantee of good feng shui. According to classical feng shui, a red door can have a protective effect in certain circumstances, and in certain other circumstances it can provide a remedy of decisive importance if the positioning of the door is in conflict with the element the house is resting on. But there are many other circumstances when a red door is the last thing you want. If you can make an exact measurement of the direction the house is facing – for instance, back to the east and front to the west – you will be able to find out on which trigram the house is resting and thus be able to paint the door a colour which belongs to the same element as the trigram or in a colour from the preceding element. If the back is to the east, the trigram for the eldest son is what we find there, and that is a wood trigram (see Chapter 2). Colours from the wood element or water element (which feeds and nourishes wood) would be a good choice – that is to say, green, turquoise, navy blue or black. The exception is when the door faces a direction which conflicts in element terms with the trigram at the back. But you will need feng shui expertise to discover this.

Remember that strong colours are yang irrespective of the element, so consider what the individual rooms are being used for. Feng shui recommends that walls are painted in mellow colours and that it is better to restrict colour effects to curtains, mouldings, furniture and so on. And even when a wall colour is subdued and neutral, it still retains its value and has power to vibrate and be influential.

Feng shui consultants who use colours, frequently loud colours, as their most important tool are better thought of as interior decoration consultants rather than as feng shui experts. Interior decoration is largely a matter of fashion trends, and in that case commercial interests are paramount.

The house and you

Even though the principles involved in balancing elements are the same when analysing a house and analysing a person, it is important not to fall into the trap of mixing two such different things as a building and a human being. A house is inhabited by several people, and there are people moving in and out of the house. But the feng shui for a house takes precedence: if, for instance, the metal element is necessary to achieve balance in a bedroom whereas your personal analysis states you need fire, you should allow the bedroom (and other rooms) to receive whatever remedies they require in terms of colour, form and so on. This solution will create the best feng shui both for you and for the other inhabitants of the house.

The personal advice you have been given will deal with the colour of your clothes, activities and careers, directions and climate and, in the case of an advanced analysis, any other adjustments which may pertain to the house and the positioning of things. If, for instance, there is a yawning gulf between your personal requirement in terms of elements and those of the bedroom – in which, after all, you spend many hours – there are other possibilities: try sleeping in bedclothes and pyjamas that are the colour that benefits you in element terms.

An experienced feng shui adviser will be able to give you other supportive and effective advice in order to achieve the best possible balance and harmony between yourself and the house you live in.

FENG SHUI CONSULTATION

No one has a perfect life and one way or another most people would benefit from professional feng shui analysis of their home. Some need it more than others, as several of the stories in this volume reveal. If, for example, you are struggling to find why your life has got stuck in a rut, whether it has to do with your career, your finances, your marital life, health or well-being, there is a significant probability that your home or its surroundings can provide a good indication of the reason. A serious, professional feng shui consultant is trained to see connections that are not immediately obvious to other people.

Feng shui has its roots in a holistic, profoundly ecological way of thinking in which every single part of the whole – large or small – counts. And the whole also includes invisible but powerful fields of energy around the place we live.

Feng shui consultants work in different ways. Some offer advice on the basis of what they see there and then at your home and are probably trained mainly to evaluate conditions involving visible forms. Others arrive with a feng shui compass and take measurements of everything from the garden gate to the positioning of your desk and bed. Both form and compass are used in classical feng shui, which means that you get a truly profound analysis.

It costs money and it takes time, so when and why should you spend your time and money on feng shui and a feng shui consultation? It takes time for the consultant or adviser to carry out the work and the advice you are asked to follow will also cost you money. There may be adaptations outside and inside, changes to the use of rooms, painting and papering and much else. You must therefore have really good reasons before calling in a feng shui adviser. An analysis can often uncover conditions and causes in the following kind of situations:

- You move somewhere new and life takes a different turn.
- You are experiencing new health issues.
- You lose your job.
- You are constantly ending up in conflict.
- You lose initiative and energy.
- You are sleeping badly.

- You are finding it difficult to conceive.
- You feel your money is running out faster than it is coming in.
- You are constantly suffering from accidents and injuries.
- You are struggling with dependency.
- You lack a partner.

There is no point in paying a lot of money for a serious feng shui consultation if what you want is some quick magic solution. In that case you would be better off buying a book of magic feng shui tips, enjoying it and being satisfied with that. But if you are curious about what feng shui can contribute to your life and you have a gut feeling that tells you that here is something you should take a serious look at, then it would be sensible to follow your intuition. It might well be that you will discover connections you would otherwise be unaware of and, as you will have understood by now, there might be serious issues at stake. We put our cars in for servicing and maintenance and there are advanced analytic techniques that can discover critical faults and save us paying large sums for repairs later. And, importantly, this maintenance also helps prevent accidents caused by brake failure and the like.

Similarly, we go and have our health checked annually by the company doctor – blood, urine, lungs, heart and much more. But when it comes to our home, we have no familiarity with the language that can provide an analysis of what is going on. All buildings need a health check, both the one you live in and the one you work in.

Carina had her apartment checked and this is what she reported back a year later:

First and foremost: I have had very little illness during the year since your visit and I have dealt with most of the things you advised me to. I no longer have stomach trouble, my blood pressure and pulse are steadier (my heart was slightly arhythmic before), and I've become more creative – that's what I notice most, perhaps.

You advised me to find some way of screening the view in from the road and I put some plants on the balcony, but I didn't feel they helped very much. What did help, though, was to change the blinds in the living room and get blinds I can draw right down on one side and thus cut out some of the view in from the street. The atmosphere in the living room is now quite different from what it was – and much better.

So, since starting to redecorate and put up the recommended colours, I haven't had much to complain about. The horoscope you did for me has been pretty accurate down to the last detail. Things were very busy at work during the winter (the horoscope said I'd have a strenuous winter), but everything went well, perhaps because the energy was better at home.

Floor plan and map of the plot
Whatever your reasons for trying feng shui may be, the first thing we do is to have a short chat about where the shoe is pinching and what it is you want. And we agree on a price and a schedule for the consultation. I ask you to provide me with a copy of the floor plan and as a rule I also ask for a map of the plot showing the house or building. At the same time I ask for the birth data of everyone who lives in the house (or for the regular manager or owner of a business).

There are some feng shui consultants who are content with the plans being sent to them and they will then send you an analysis, along with advice and explanations. And a bill. People who do that and call it feng shui must have an unbelievably well-developed sixth sense, because to do feng shui fully and properly, it is essential for the consultant to turn up with all five senses working: they are much more important than any sixth sense.

When I arrive to do feng shui for a client, I always spend a lot of time outside the house. There is nothing mystical and ritualistic about what I am doing: I am working actively to observe everything that might have some sort of influence on the house and those who live there. I look at the energy flow to the house, assess whether the building has sufficient support on all sides, see what any missing supports or corners of the building might have to tell me of the more universal truths about the trigrams inside and outside and what this might mean for each and every one of those who live in the house.

I use the feng shui compass and take measurements, which I also do indoors. I work through the entrance area, the hall and all the other rooms in the house, noting everything of significance for the work of analysis I shall concentrate on during the days following the consultation.

The client is more than welcome to be present, and that is an advantage for me as I will certainly have questions to ask along the way. I also offer concrete advice as I go along – on the use of mirrors, for instance, or the positioning of beds, or the importance of support where you sleep or sit and work. I am not bothered whether the house is scrubbed and polished when I arrive. Of course, the flow in the house is better when it is clean and tidy, but there are many other things that determine the kind of feng shui – good or bad – that people surround themselves with.

No one house is like another, no life is like another. Business premises in the same street can experience success and failure.

As a rule, feng shui will almost always come up with the reason. If you desire children but lack 'child energy' at the bedroom door or in the double bed, a compass measurement can help to change the situation, always assuming you are willing to follow the advice you are given. If you feel that things are working against you at work, if you feel that you are not getting support for you and yours in life, we can look to see whether your house or apartment has good enough support and is therefore capable of providing sufficient support to those who live there. There is always a connection and there is always a way to make an intervention.

Written report

I will then provide you with a report in which I describe my discoveries. I will give you an evaluation of the connections I have seen and the calculations I have made to provide us with information about the basic energies of the house and the time-based, invisible element influences in your house in particular. The analysis and report are normally ready within a week or two of my visit.

You will be given advice and recommendations as to what you should do in the house and why you should do it. It may sometimes be to paint a particular room in a particular colour, or to move to a different bedroom, or to turn the home office into a bedroom and vice versa. Using special measurements, I may find the reason why 'money seems to disappear with the speed of light': you may need to adjust a door frame to allow the door to receive more favourable energy and thereby contribute to putting your economy on a sounder footing. It might be that there is a mirror reinforcing unfavourable energy, or it may be that misfortune, reverses and concrete health problems can, in a variety of ways, be read from the house and are a result of its architecture and construction. If the issues that emerge are serious ones, it may be necessary to make structural changes to the building.

In some situations there will be a great deal to be done and some of the things may demand significant investment. I always attempt to find simple and sensible solutions to start with and hope that they lead to an improved flow, more energy and effort and better finances, which in turn will open the way to undertaking more major changes.

In the case of a business, the location of the employees is important, and the kind of location in which the management works is of decisive importance. It is also important to assess the type of business and the connections with the five elements, form and colours. Yet again, measurements are of great significance: is 'money energy' coming in through the door of the business? A shop needs customers and if the right energy does not come to the door business can be sluggish and customers may prefer the shop next door or the one over the road. Some businesses suffer not only from competition in the vicinity but also from unfavourable energy directly at their door – in which case the business is frequently doing badly. Sometimes a very small adjustment will do the trick: examine the positioning of the counter and till, consider repositioning things or refurnishing, look at the choice of office and desk position of the financial manager. Moving the position of the counter and the till will very often lead to a significant increase in turnover.

I have carried out feng shui on many different businesses, from medical clinics, offices and manufacturing enterprises to shops, both large and small. Frequently, for instance, there have been issues of conflict between employees and management, and there is also the desire to increase the turnover. It is a splendid feeling when your client telephones a week later and joyfully informs you that the till never stops ringing.

Here is the story of Nina Liseth who runs In-spire, a combined interior decoration, flower and clothes shop and, as if that wasn't enough, she runs a café, pavilion and reception room at the same premises. Her husband runs an electrical business in the same building. The couple also have three children. Complicated logistics are called for to get all of this to fit together and most of us would be run ragged by less. And then, additionally, there is the financial aspect and turnover to think about. The premises are halfway between Florø and Førde, two small towns in a remote area, so rather off the beaten track, so how to go about catching people's attention and getting customers to turn in?

We discussed ideas about how to make a direct and quite brazen use of the main road to create interest and get motorists to turn off and come in, and to use the same advertising hoardings to attract attention to the premises. The logos of the two firms needed a thorough rethink and there were a great many purely practical things to be done to get the place to function better for customers and for employees. The compass measurements revealed a slightly worrying energy in Nina's part of the premises – a type of energy that often leads to shops or houses constantly changing hands. This was the most important thing for me to attend to and I hoped she would prioritise it.

In-spire

I first encountered feng shui in 2014 when a good friend of mine wanted to arrange an introductory course with Reni in Florø.

My husband and I are in business independently and we were curious whether Reni could help us to give the businesses a boost and use feng shui to guide us through changes that could have an effect on our hectic and labour-intensive daily lives. We looked on it as a financial investment in the future, both in a personal sense and for our businesses.

When we received the report, I read it with the feeling that 'Yes, this is exactly the way things should be!' I felt that Reni had pointed out many things that my husband and I had discussed without being able to put our fingers on quite what it was we sensed. That the solutions and changes she was pointing out were obvious, though we hadn't seen them. But with the curtain pulled aside, all was revealed.

Some of the changes Reni suggested have already been done; others are more financially demanding and we shall look at them over a longer timescale. In February of this year we undertook some restructuring in the premises where we operate the florist's, the interior decor and fashion boutique as well as the café and the reception room (it's enough to make you breathless). Since then we have had a 'natural' cut in the number of staff and we are now doing the same job with half as many employees, while our system and oversight of the business is actually better than before. In addition to that we have made changes to our profile and that will pay off in the long term.

As a recently established entrepreneur with plenty of drive and a heavy workload for many years, I found it unbelievably valuable to have the support that this discipline – represented by Reni – has to offer. I am certain that the businesses we run will develop well and that there will be an improvement in our everyday home life, where we gather our energy and come together for pleasure and socialisation with friends and family. – *Nina Liseth, In-spire AS*

Following it up

Once a client, always a client – if that is what you want! You will be given an explanation of everything you don't understand immediately, and there certainly will be things that you don't understand since feng shui involves foreign words and a very foreign language. I will go through the report and the findings and explain and justify the suggestions I am making. It's possible that the house needs a boost in energy terms or Buddha support (see page 104), in which case good and appropriate timing is important. This means that my consultation includes suggestions as to a favourable day and hour at which the things should be done or changes made. As was said earlier, feng shui is about both time and space.

My favourite clients are those who constantly contact me with new questions, send me enthusiastic reports on what has been done (tidying up, repainting, extending, ordering new doors and so on), accompanied by photographic evidence of what they have proudly achieved. Sometimes there are also rapid reports of the changes taking place in their lives, but it usually takes some time before results become obvious. The energy has to settle in order to get an opportunity to work. On occasion this happens quickly and the client is able to see the direct connection between the feng shui process and the changes in his or her life; at other times it can take so long that feng shui is not given so much credit for the change.

After a year it will be possible to determine whether the house has benefited and existence has changed for those who live there. This is the time for renewed contact and further follow-up. Every single year posits new influences in energy terms (time energy again!) for every building. If they have their personal feng shui adviser, anyone who wants to know the challenges and opportunities ahead, whether for their home or for their business, from month to month and year to year, has the chance to find out.

WORDS AND CONCEPTS

Here are a number of words and phrases you will frequently encounter in books and web pages about feng shui. Most of them also occur in this book.

ba chop: see basic energies.

ba gua: 'eight house' is a pattern with nine squares, eight of which refer to the directions and the ninth, in the middle, is the centre (of a property, a house, or a room). Gua is also known as 'kwa' and indicates the trigram in every direction. Ba gua can also mean 'eight hooks', in which case it is referring to an old Chinese tradition from the days when the wise men of a village would hang up predictions about current and future events on eight hooks on the village square. Ba gua has also become the popular term for the simplified method of dividing a dwelling into areas to do with different aspects of human life. This is also called 'simple ba gua' or 'Western ba gua' and is not used in classical feng shui.

basic energies: cosmic energies have their equivalents here on Earth. Each of the stars in the Plough is in harmony with a mountain form on Earth, and in all houses there are eight different (invisible) forms of energy arranged in different constellations. Half of them are good and the other half are challenging. Where an invisible negative energy form is accompanied by the same type of form, either within a house (piece of furniture, figure, picture) or outside as a concrete physical form (mountain, ridge, hedge, tree, roof ridge, etc.), the influence will be reinforced and will have an impact on the lives of the inhabitants. The same holds true, of course, for good influences. The method for revealing this is called 'ba chop'.

Buddha support: energy support for a building when measurements taken at the back of the house reveal that the energy is insufficiently strong. A supportive Buddha statue should be of a certain weight and size – after all, it has to have a strengthening influence on a whole house. Ideally speaking, it should be located outside, but a Buddha support inside is also possible. It should be positioned by someone knowledgeable about feng shui, who can locate the correct position and also the correct time for putting it in place. As a rule, a statue of Buddha is used, but there is nothing to prevent the use of some other kind of spiritual symbol.

cardinal direction: heaven direction, one of the four main directions: north, south, east and west.

chi: life energy, life force, the breath of life, universal energy (prana, ki, nipi, etc.); a concept that is not well known in our culture but which is being used more frequently as Eastern healing methods, philosophy and world view become closer and more familiar to us.

Chue: Chue feng shui (or Chue Style feng shui) is a classical style of feng shui taught by Grand Master Chan Kun Wah. Over time it has come to have the mark of quality in Europe, where there are now over a thousand consultants educated in this style. It is named after the Taoist feng shui master Chue Yuen, who is famous for his accomplishments in Hong Kong and all over the Far East. His knowledge of feng shui is based on powerful ancient methods and he chose Grand Master Chan Kun Wah as the sole heir to his treasure trove of wisdom.

compass school: the variety of feng shui that reads and interprets directions. Effective and almost 'surgical', but only fully useful when used in conjunction with the effects of form. Working with form and compass are not two competing approaches to feng shui; they are two sides of the same thing: they complement one another and contribute to powerful results. The compass work involves reading the effects of energy at all 360 degrees around a house (see also lo pan).

dragon support: an elevation in the terrain, another building, a thick hedge, etc. on the left-hand side of the house when you are standing in front of the house looking outwards. The 'dragon side' has to do with the male aspects of existence and with support/lack of support for the man of the house.

early heaven: the sequence in which the trigrams are in an original order – heaven is in its place and earth is in its place. Fire and water are in perfect balance (see also later heaven).

electromagnetic stress: stress caused by radiation from electrical or digital sources. Feng shui recommends that you should avoid exposing yourself to this in rooms where you spend any great length of time – as, for instance, in the bedroom.

feng shui: 'wind water' – a relatively new term for an ancient discipline. Feng shui means 'energy': in practical life it means finding ways to utilise good 'winds' and to ensure there is protection against the bad. We all prefer fresh, life-enhancing water and try to avoid water that is stagnant, dirty, dark and dangerous. In feng shui all of this is translated into the effects of energy, which we attempt to arrange as far as possible to benefit the fresh, life-enhancing, pure energy that gives us opportunities in life. (Notice by the way that feng shui is written in the lower case, as are heaven directions, bicycle stands, yoga, meditation and school breakfast; not capitalised as are Coca Cola, Volvo or John Smith.)

feng shui compass: see lo pan.

five elements: the cycle of life, the cycle of day and night, the cycles of the seasons, the heaven directions, time and much more can be broken up into five steps in a process that follows a definite pattern. Knowledge of this process underlies the Chinese theory of the five elements – wood, fire, earth, metal, water.

five heavenly animals: 'heaven on earth' – protective landforms around a place of residence. The question of support or no support is one of the most important questions in feng shui! The house needs support at its back (tortoise support), it needs support on each side (tiger and dragon support), and it needs support in front (phoenix support). The fifth heavenly animal is called the snake or the yellow dragon and it represents a well and harmoniously positioned house.

flow: something we all desire in life is for things to go our way. Very often it is precisely things that put barriers along our road. When a home is piled high with a thousand things, life becomes too crowded: you put on weight, feel that everything is hard-going, can't make progress, can't carry through projects and so on. A lack of flow often leads to a lack of time because you can't find what you are looking for or have to spend a great deal of time and energy taking care of the things you possess.

flying stars: a phrase you will see in many different presentations of feng shui. Stars that fly? The concept is referring to heaven energies, that is cosmic influences (like, for instance, the importance of the moon for the tides on our planet). Using certain techniques, it is possible for a feng shui expert to reveal how these elemental influences affect a place of residence. It deals with the five elements that constantly position themselves in new ways in different major feng shui periods; and they affect houses in different ways depending on the direction the house faces. Each year one of the elements will have a stronger influence than the rest and that can reinforce the effect of the element in different rooms in the house.

form school: the primary knowledge of feng shui deals with the surroundings of a house, the land forms and supporting structures and the influence they exert.

Grand Master Chan Kun Wah: the founder of the Imperial School of Feng Shui and Chinese Horoscopes and teacher of authentic classical feng shui. He started his career in feng shui as young as 14, handpicked by Chue Yan, one of the most knowledgeable feng shui masters of modern times. Chue's strong desire for the survival of the discipline of feng shui led him to command his sole pupil to move to Europe and begin to educate Western students. Over a thousand people in Europe have now undergone basic education in Chue Style feng shui. Grand Master Chan is resident in Scotland and in Hong Kong.

gua: or kwa, are Chinese words for trigrams and hexagram (see the following entry). A trigram is a small gua and a hexagram a big gua.

hexagram: six lines, broken and/or unbroken. A hexagram is composed of two trigrams (see trigram). Among other things, the 64 hexagrams tell us about the energy in each of the directions and they thus provide important knowledge for the feng shui expert. The hexagrams, which are gathered together in the I Ching (see entry below), are also called the DNA of the universe and are said to contain information about absolutely everything around us and within us.

I Ching: ancient wisdom texts regarding change and the nature of change; an ancient text that dates back many thousands of years in China and which has undergone changes through the ages. A collection of signs (trigrams and hexagrams) and wisdom texts. This body of knowledge is the very foundation of the classic feng shui discipline. Even today the I Ching is used as an oracle and can provide answers on everything from health and family increase to negotiations and diplomacy. The I Ching is used particularly assiduously in the world of finance!

later heaven: the sequence which shows how the trigrams position themselves inside every building, with each of the elements in the heaven direction that corresponds to how we humans perceive the order of things: fire in the south, water in the north and so on (see also early heaven).

lo pan: the feng shui compass, which is used to measure the effects of energy around and in a house. It is composed of a series of rings that contain information about everything relevant to a feng shui analysis. In the centre is a compass needle that shows magnetic north.

lo shu: the numbers from 1 to 9 placed in a particular order on a grid (see ba gua) with the number 5 in the middle. The pattern is said to be derived from the shell of an enormous tortoise that rose from the River Luo after a violent flood. The pattern and the numbers are called the 'magic square' (see below) and are used in feng shui to reveal what is happening in energy terms in the different directions in a house.

macrocosm: the macrocosm and the microcosm are often used in the sense that mankind is a small world (microcosm) that mirrors the great world, the universe.

magic square: the numbers from 1 to 9 placed in a grid in which the sum is 15 in all directions. The odd numbers lie in the cardinal directions (across the middle) and the even numbers lie in the corners (the sub-cardinal directions). It is used in the flying stars technique in feng shui (space and time).

microcosm: see macrocosm.

ming tang: directly translated it means 'bright hall', that is to say, the area in front of the house which according to feng shui should be open and light and preferably with a view.

mirrors: mirrors reflect objects for 24 hours a day, so you need to be careful about what the mirror is thereby reinforcing: piles of shoes and rubbish, or a picture of something you don't really want to have in your life? Mirrors placed incorrectly in the entrance part of the house can bounce energy back out again. And, importantly, mirrors reflect invisible as well as visible energies, so be careful how you use them.

Plough: a well-known and well-loved constellation of stars in the sky. It resembles a plough or small cart, but also a ladle or dipper. Seamen have used it throughout the ages as a safe guide to sail by. Taking two of the stars in the Plough as your starting point, it is easy to locate the Pole Star. The handle of the ladle always points in the direction that represents the season we are in. Feng shui uses knowledge of the influence the macrocosm has on our minute microcosm to reveal what kind of energies pertain in and around buildings (see basic energies).

poison arrow: a threatening structure, a pointed shape. In Chinese a poison arrow is called sat chi or sha chi. We should avoid being subjected to poison arrows anywhere we spend long periods of time – in the bedroom, for instance, or where we are sitting working. And the house should not have that kind of threatening shape aimed at its back (the spine, the middle of the back) or at the entrance door.

sang chi: life-giving energy; the nourishing and beneficial energy we desire to bring into a place of residence and which it is best to sleep in.

sat chi: poisonous and negative energy, also called a 'poison arrow'. Sat chi can be everything from – quite literally – a threatening arrow (that is to say, a pointed formation, a corner or an edge) to ugly lamp-posts, transformers, unpleasant noise or disturbing light. Or it might be a threatening river, poor maintenance or a rotten smell.

seal of Saturn: one of many universal patterns that reveal magic combinations of numbers. The pattern in the seal of Saturn is followed in the flying star technique (see flying stars and also lo shu).

shamanism: Not many people associate feng shui with shamanism – not until they have immersed themselves in classical feng shui, that is. Feng shui offers the knowledge and a language that makes it possible to understand and communicate better with nature and its cycles and processes. The shamans in ancient times possessed that kind of insight; they observed, they looked upwards to observe the sky and they looked downwards from the mountaintops because this gave the necessary overview. Feng shui, in the way it developed in China over many thousands of years, is thought to have its origins in the Siberian shamanic tradition.

space clearing: this covers everything from spring cleaning, tidying up and throwing things out to more ritual forms of cleansing rooms. You can use soap, water and fresh air, and you can use candles, incense, essential oils, sea salt, music, drums, bells, songs and dance. Cleansing is important after sickness, arguments or shocks and is an excellent thing to do in connection with the transitions between the seasons.

sub-cardinal direction: the intermediate directions – north-east, south-east, south-west and north-west. In energy terms the sub-cardinal direction is more mixed than the pure cardinal direction and therefore more complex and challenging (see cardinal direction).

Taoism: One of the three main religious traditions that have formed Chinese culture over the last three thousand years. Its spiritual ideal is anchored in a mythic prehistory when people lived in a simple state in close contact with nature.

tiger support: a landform or a building on the right-hand side of the house when you are standing in front of it looking outwards. A good tiger takes care of female characteristics and values and provides the woman of the house with support in energy terms.

tortoise support: the kind of support we like to see behind a building, particularly as an elevation in the landscape, though these days it is more likely to be a neighbour's house that provides tortoise support. A good solid hedge or fence can also provide the house with support and protection.

trigram: three lines, either broken or unbroken, yin or yang. The three lines also represent earth, man and heaven.

wind chimes: metal or bamboo tubes hanging freely so that the wind causes them to strike each other and chime.

yin and yang: two opposite universal forces which are simultaneously mutually dependent.

yuen hom: the mystery of the void, from nothing to everything. In feng shui, the art of making the impossible possible.

FURTHER READING

Chue Style is acknowledged as one of the most valid styles of feng shui to be practised in the world today. You can find consultants and schools in many countries. The Chue Foundation website will give you the total overview: www.chuefoundation.org

I Ching or Book of Changes
Foreword by Carl Gustav Jung. Translation: Richard Wilhelm, Penguin Books

Lao Tzu: *Tao te Ching*

Thomas F. Aylward: *The Imperial Guide to Feng Shui & Chinese Astrology*, Watkinson Publishing

Pamela Ferguson: *Take Five. The Five Elements Guide to Health and Harmony*, Newleaf

Zaihong Shen: *Feng Shui: Harmonizing Your Inner & Outer Space*, Dorling Kindersley

Michael Warden: *Design Energetics: The Ancient Pulse of Feng Shui in the Modern World*, self-published

Ewa Wong: *Feng-Shui. The Ancient Wisdom of Harmonius Living for Modern Times*, Shambala

Ewa Wong: *A Master Course in Feng-Shui*, Shambala

CLOSING WORDS

My purpose in writing this book has been to show that feng shui is not a 'do-it-yourself' matter. I hope that after having read it you will have recognised what a huge influence the house and its surroundings have on the lives we live.

Having an insight into feng shui opens the way to greater consciousness of the interdependence of all things, and for many people this will be the start of a journey – a journey undertaken in a new state of awareness. I hope each and every one of you has this experience.

In reality, feng shui is about everything, but it is also almost impossible to generalise because every individual, every home and every situation is unique. In traditional Chinese thought and understanding, a person is never looked at in isolation from his or her fate and feng shui. Everything a human being experiences in life is unique, every building is unique, and the way an individual and a house combine is unique.

On the journey we call life it is easy for trivialities to take over – bad weather, car brands, varieties of wine, tidying up, fashions, neighbours, celebrities – especially when basic needs have been taken care of and the horizon isn't filled with threatening clouds. Knowledge of feng shui awakens in us a new consciousness of who we – as human beings – are in the great scheme, halfway between heaven and earth.

There could be no more fitting closing words than the following exhortation, taken from the Tao Te Ching, the work of wisdom concerning 'the way':

Try to understand the force that is yang –
But in your essence be more yin.
Be like a valley
As it opens out for the river,
Be like a river
For the earth...
And lead it in its right bed
So that it flows towards the sea.
Be newborn – be free from yourself,
Be humble,
Be close to the earth
Be a valley for the whole world.